Growing with MATHEMATICS

FIFTH GRADE

DISCUSSION BOOK

MIMOSA
Education

Authors	Calvin J. Irons, Ph.D. Thomas E. Rowan, Ph.D.
Mathematics Editor	Claire Owen
Design	Gordon Hill, Peter Shaw
Consultants	Laurie Godwin Assistant Principal Aurora Public Schools, Aurora, CO
	Eileen Harris, Ph.D. Director of Planning and Evaluation Charlotte County School District, Port Charlotte, FL
	Mari Muri Mathematics Consultant Connecticut State Department of Education, Hartford, CT
	Barbara Ramsey Curriculum Resource Teacher – Math and Science Santee School District, Santee, CA
	Michelle Rohr Director of Mathematics Houston Independent School District, Houston, TX

Acknowledgments

The authors are grateful to everyone who participated in the development of this project.
Special thanks go to the following:
Robyn Platt, Jean Rasmussen, Brigid Rasmussen, Christie Cycles, and
for appearing in photographs:
Robyn Platt, Darryl Snr., Darryl Jnr., Derrick, and Darren McDonald, Michael and Kate Owen, Emily Johns, Alison Moon, James Poladoris, Annette and Michael Petidis, Natalie Pattuwage, Rachel Luria, Inga Gonzalez

Published in the United States of America by
MIMOSA EDUCATION
50 South Steele Street
Denver, Colorado 80209
1-800-MIMOSA-1
1-800-646-672-1

ISBN 1 5769 9029 x
Color reproduction by Tricolor Graphic
Printed in Hong Kong
10 9 8 7 6 5

Contents

1. Look at the picture and list all the different numbers you see. What does each number refer to?

2. How many CDs do you think the store would sell in an average week? How did you make your estimate? What are some other questions you could ask about the number of CDs the store sells?

3. 100,000 CDs could be displayed on 40 stands, each holding 2,500 CDs. What are some other ways a store could display 100,000 CDs?

4. If 100 staff are needed to work the three shifts on a Saturday, how many might work on each shift?
   a. 6 a.m. – 2 p.m.   **b.** 2 p.m. – 10 p.m.   **c.** 10 p.m. – 6 a.m.

5. Make up some other mathematical questions about the information in the picture.

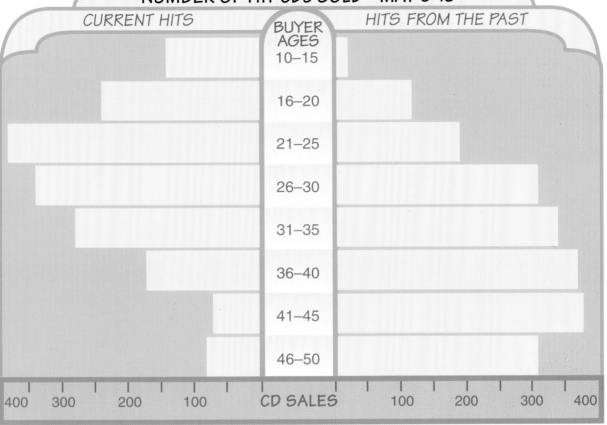

MUSIC WAREHOUSE
NUMBER OF HIT CDs SOLD – MAY 6-13

CURRENT HITS | BUYER AGES | HITS FROM THE PAST

	10–15	
	16–20	
	21–25	
	26–30	
	31–35	
	36–40	
	41–45	
	46–50	

400 300 200 100 CD SALES 100 200 300 400

1. What does the graph tell you?

2. Who bought the greatest number of:
   a. current hits?   b. hits from the past?   c. total hits?

3. Look at the data for each age group. Try to explain the differences in buying patterns among the age groups.

4. The Music Warehouse managers are placing an order for 1,000 hit CDs.
   a. How could you use the graph to help them decide which kind of CDs to order?
   b. How many CDs of each type do you think they should order?

5. Use the graph to make up some other questions.

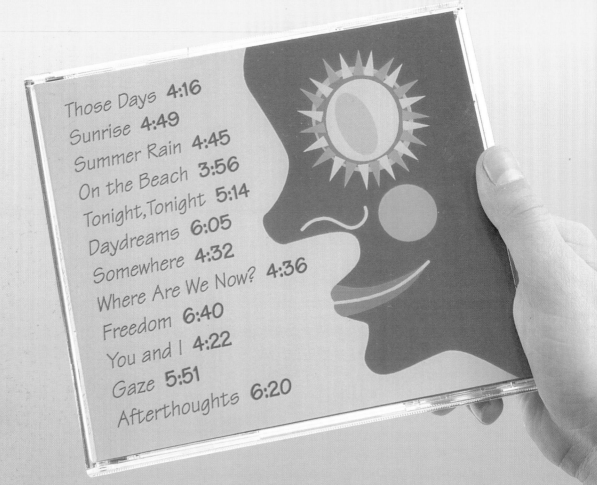

Those Days 4:16
Sunrise 4:49
Summer Rain 4:45
On the Beach 3:56
Tonight, Tonight 5:14
Daydreams 6:05
Somewhere 4:32
Where Are We Now? 4:36
Freedom 6:40
You and I 4:22
Gaze 5:51
Afterthoughts 6:20

1. Which song is closest to:

   a. 4 minutes? **b.** $4\frac{1}{2}$ minutes? **c.** $5\frac{1}{4}$ minutes?

2. Is the total length of the first 2 songs more or less than 9 minutes? How do you know?

3. Choose 2 songs which have a total playing time of about 10 minutes. How many combinations can you find?

4. Estimate the total playing time of the CD. How did you make your estimate?

5. If the CD is played in order, which song will be playing:

   a. 30 minutes after the start? **b.** 45 minutes after the start?

6. Find another CD. Is the total playing time more or less than the CD shown above?

MIX AND MATCH CD STACKS

CD TOWER 1 by 96

1. Which stack holds the most CDs?
   How did you figure it out?

2. Why do you think they are called
   Mix and Match Stacks?

3. If you had 150 CDs, which stacks would you buy
   to store them in? (They don't have to fill the stacks.)
   How did you mix and match the stacks?

4. What is the greatest number of CDs these
   people can store in their stacks?
   a. Sarah has 5 CD Starters.   **b.** Gina has 3 CD Duos.
   c. Ryan has 4 CD Triples.

5. Can you find another way for each person above
   to buy stacks to store the same number of CDs?
   How would you do it?

6. Design a stack that would hold 128 CDs.

CD DUO 2 by 32

CD TRIPLE 3 by 16

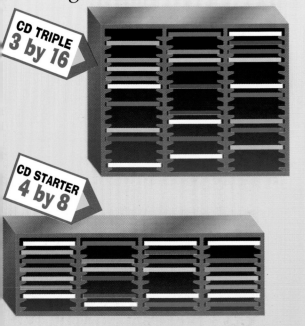

CD STARTER 4 by 8

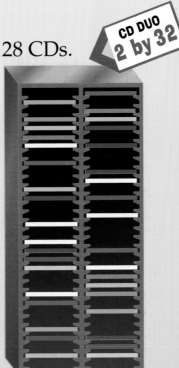

a.

b.

c.

d.

1. Look at each picture. What shapes do you see?

2. For each 3-dimensional shape, what **surfaces** are:
   a. curved?   **b.** flat?

3. What 2-dimensional shapes do you see that have:
   a. straight edges?   **b.** curved edges?

4. Look at the pictures again. What circles and parts of circles do you see?

5. List some other places where you can see circles.

1. What are Katy and Ben using to draw their circle?
   What tool does the same job?

   a. How would you instruct someone to draw a circle using Katy and Ben's tools?

   b. What directions would you give for drawing a square?

   c. Which is easier to draw, a circle or a square? Explain why.

2. What is the meaning of each of these words?
   a. *circumference*
   b. *diameter*
   c. *radius*
   (You can use the pictures to help.)

   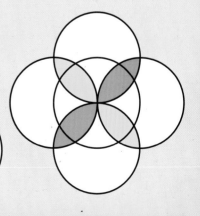

   The distance from any point on a circle to the center is called the *radius*. In Latin, radius means a "spoke."

3. Experiment with your compass to make these patterns. Record the steps you used.

   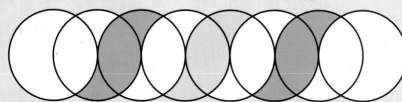

Sophie and Larry searched the Internet for information on circles. This is one piece of information they found.

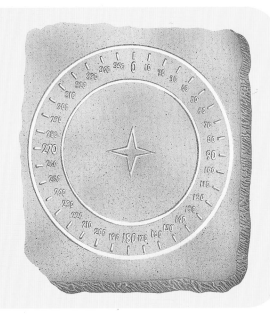

MATHNET

The Babylonians believed that the sun circled the Earth every 360 days. So, to measure around a circle, they divided the circumference into 360 equal parts. These parts, called degrees, are still used as a unit of measurement for circles and angles.

Use what you have learned about the number of degrees in a circle to describe the movement of the minute hand around a clock.

1. How far will the minute hand move after these times? Give your answers as a fraction of a circle and then in degrees.

   a. 15 minutes **b.** 30 minutes

   c. 45 minutes **d.** 60 minutes

   What did you discover?

2. If the minute hand has moved $\frac{1}{3}$ of the way around the clock:

   a. How many minutes has it passed?

   b. Through how many degrees has it moved?

3. How can you use fractions of a circle to help you figure out degrees?

Sophie and Larry used their protractors
to measure angles of a triangle.

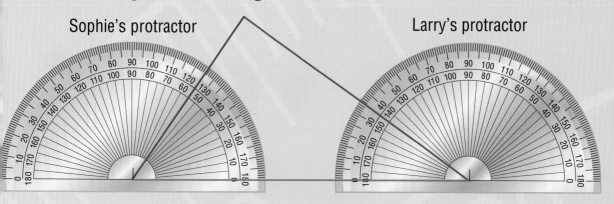

Sophie's protractor   Larry's protractor

1. Look at the protractors.
   What do you notice about the two sets of numbers on each?

2. Look at the angle that Larry is measuring.
   a. Is that angle greater or smaller than 90 degrees?
   b. Which set of numbers would you use to measure it? Why?
   c. How many degrees are between the red and the blue lines?
   d. Explain how you know that your answer makes sense.

3. Now look at the angle that Sophie is measuring.
   She said that it measured 125 degrees.
   a. Do you think Sophie was correct?
      How do you know?
   b. How many degrees are between
      the red and the green lines?

4. Is the angle Sophie measured larger or smaller than Larry's
   angle? What is the total number of degrees in the 2 angles?

5. How many degrees do you think are in the angle between the
   green and blue lines? Use a protractor to check.

6. What is the total number of degrees in all 3 angles?

1. What is the size of the center angle shown between the red and green arrows in each shape?

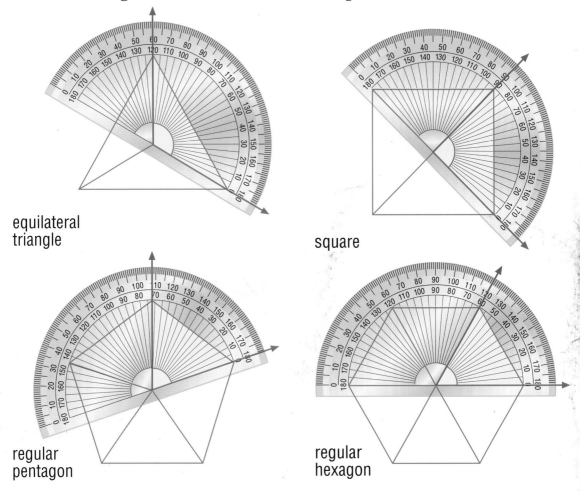

equilateral
triangle

square

regular
pentagon

regular
hexagon

2. What do you notice about the size of the **other** center angles in each shape?

3. Copy and complete this chart. What patterns do you see?

4. What do you predict for a regular 8-sided shape and a regular 10-sided shape? How could you prove it?

CENTER ANGLES

Shape	Number of angles	Measure of each angle	Total of all angles
△	3	120°	360°
▢	4	90°	
⬠	5		
⬡			

1. Look at the 2 quilt pieces. How are they the same? How are they different?

2. Measure the length of the base on each quilt piece. What do you notice?

3. Compare other matching lines on the 2 shapes. What do you notice?

4. Are the 2 shapes **congruent**? Why or why not?

5. Are the 2 shapes **similar**? How do you know?

6. Choose a matching angle at the base of each quilt piece and measure the 2 angles. What did you discover?

7. Compare other matching angles on both quilt pieces.

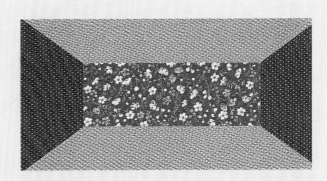

8. What have you discovered about lengths in similar shapes? … angles in similar shapes?

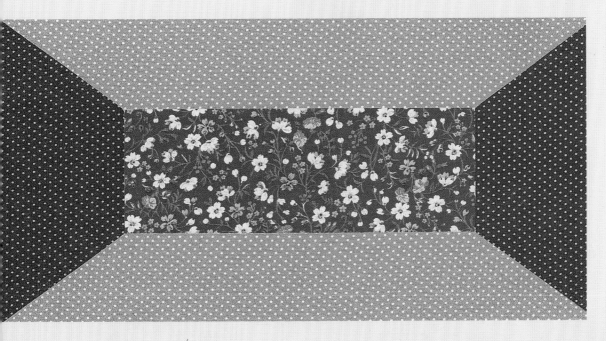

Sophie and Larry made factor sticks to help them find **common factors**.

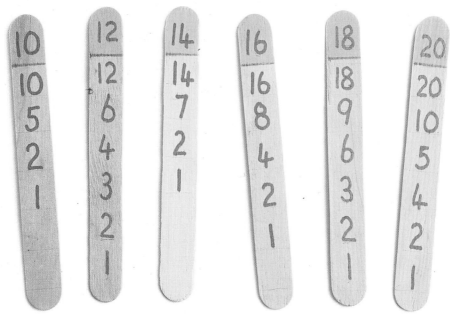

1. How do you think Sophie and Larry found all the factors of the number at the top of each stick?

2. Look at the factor sticks above.
   a. What factors are common to both 12 and 18?
   b. What is the **highest common factor** of 12 and 18?

3. Describe the steps you would follow to find the highest common factor of 24 and 28.

4. List the factors of each of the following numbers: 22, 24, 26, 28, 30.

5. Work in groups. Make factor sticks for all numbers from 10 through 30. Use your sticks to find the highest common factors for different pairs of numbers.

Zia's Pizza

	Large	Jumbo
Hawaiian Supreme	$ 7.80	$ 9.60
Daily Special	$ 9.00	$ 11.40
Mexican Special	$10.20	$ 12.60
Meat Lovers' Choice	$13.80	$15.60
All American	$15.00	$16.80

. Choose a large pizza from the board. If 3 people shared the cost of that pizza, how much would they each pay? Explain how you figured it out.

. Suppose 4 people bought the pizza you chose. Estimate each person's share of the cost. How did you make your estimate?

. Choose one jumbo pizza. What would each person's share of the cost be if:
   a. 3 people split the pizza?   **b.** 4 people split the pizza?

. Choose 2 large pizzas for 6 people to share. What are some different ways you could figure out each person's share of the cost?

. Imagine you are planning a pizza party for 8 people. Each person will contribute $4.50. List the pizzas you would buy, and figure out the amount of change each person would get back from their $4.50.

1. Pat and her friends played Peanut Pick Up. Pat recorded her results for 8 turns.

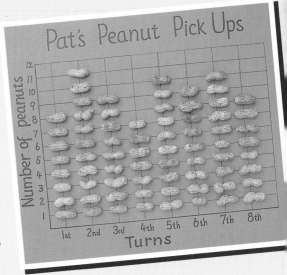

   a. What was the range of numbers for Pat's 8 turns?

   b. If Pat was asked for the number of peanuts she picked up in one turn, what number could she give? Why did you choose that number?

   c. Calculate the **mean** number of peanuts she picked up.

2. Look at the juice picture.

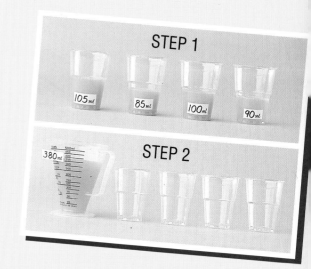

   a. In Step 2, how much juice has been poured from the 4 glasses into the measuring cup?

   b. How would you find the amount of juice to pour into each glass so they all hold the same amount?

3. How would you calculate the mean weight of these apples?

4. Work in groups with apples and peanuts.

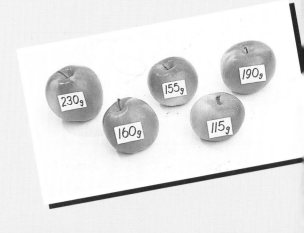

   a. What is the mean weight of your group's apples?

   b. Experiment to find the mean number of peanuts you picked up in 8 turns.

1. The Jimenez family decided to pay for their new television set in 6 equal monthly installments. What should they pay each month? How did you figure it out?

JO'S LOANS
INTEREST-FREE
Prices include sales tax

$870

2. If the Jimenez family spread their payments over 60 months, how much would they pay each month? Explain how you know.

3. Jo offers 2 payment plans for each item on sale. Calculate the monthly payment for each item using both plans. Show more than one way to figure out the amount paid each month.

$390

$560

a. Choose: 3-month plan *or* 30-month plan

b. Choose: 4-month plan *or* 40-month plan

$675

$1590

c. Choose: 5-month plan *or* 50-month plan

d. Choose: 6-month plan *or* 60-month plan

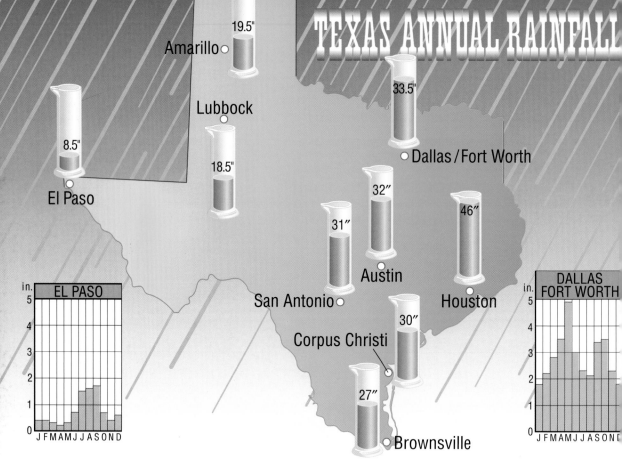

TEXAS ANNUAL RAINFALL

Amarillo ○ 19.5"

Lubbock ○

El Paso 8.5"

Dallas/Fort Worth ○ 33.5"

18.5"

San Antonio ○ 31"

Austin 32"

Houston ○ 46"

Corpus Christi ○ 30"

Brownsville ○ 27"

EL PASO (in.)

DALLAS FORT WORTH (in.)

1. Look at the rainfall for the cities on the map. Where are the driest cities? Where are the cities with the greatest rainfall?

2. What comparison questions could you ask about the rainfall in El Paso and Dallas/Fort Worth?

3. Write the rainfall for the 9 cities in order from greatest to least. Which city's rainfall is in the middle?

4. What is the mean rainfall for the 9 cities?
   How does the mean compare to the middle number?

5. Find out the annual amount of rainfall or precipitation for the place where you live.
   a. Draw a graph to show the amount that falls each month.
   b. Find the mean rainfall.
   c. List the months that have rainfall below the mean.

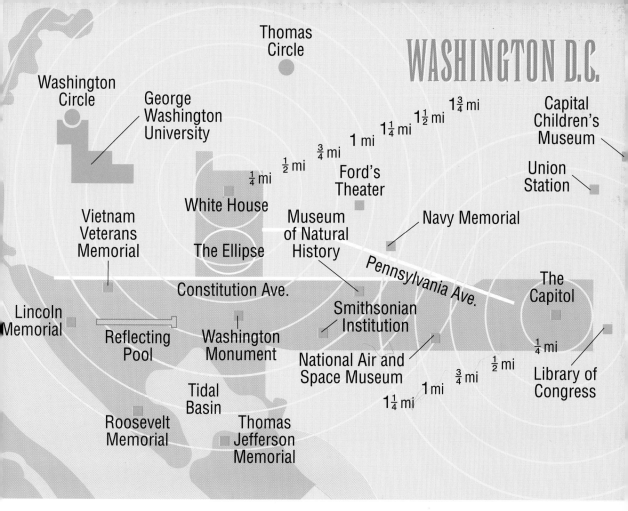

Washington D.C.

1. Look at the map of Washington D.C.
   a. Name the places at the center of the 2 sets of yellow circles.
   b. What do the circles tell you?

2. Name at least 2 buildings or monuments that are between
   ½ mile and 1 mile:
   a. from the White House   b. from the Capitol

3. What are some buildings or monuments that are about
   the same distance from the White House and the Capitol?

4. Estimate the straight line distance between:
   a. the Lincoln Memorial and the White House
   b. the White House and the Capitol
   c. Washington Circle and the Capitol

Arlene and Cory wore pedometers to measure the distance they walked in a work day.

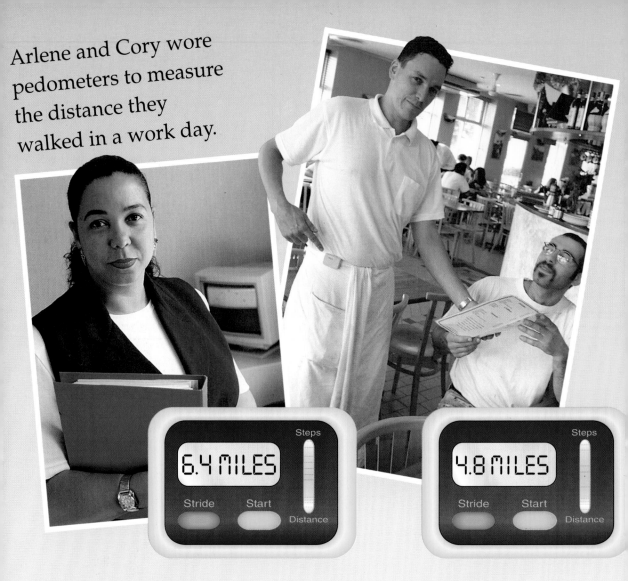

6.4 MILES   Steps   Stride   Start   Distance

4.8 MILES   Steps   Stride   Start   Distance

1. Arlene and Cory's pedometers show how far they each walked in an 8-hour day. How could you compare the distances they walked?

2. What do you think the difference in the distances would be for a 40-hour week? Explain how you made your prediction.

3. If Arlene and Cory continued to walk the same distances each week, what do you think the difference would be in:
   a. 6 months?   b. 12 months?

4. Compare the average distance per hour. Explain how you arrived at your answer.

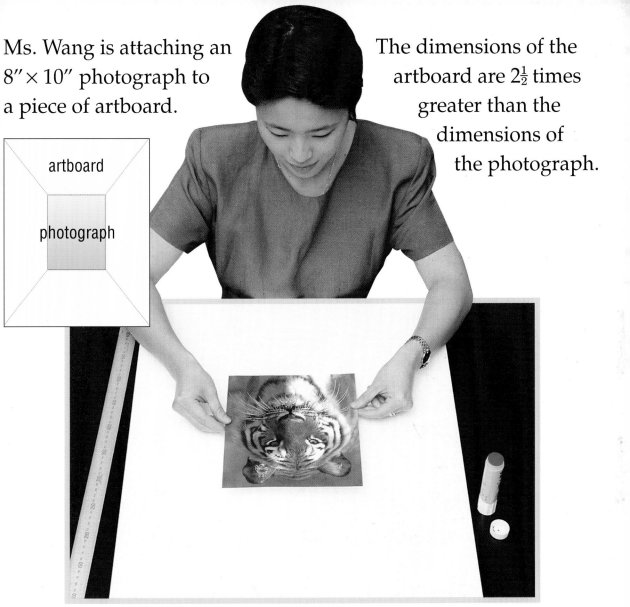

Ms. Wang is attaching an 8″ × 10″ photograph to a piece of artboard.

The dimensions of the artboard are 2½ times greater than the dimensions of the photograph.

artboard

photograph

1. What is the length of the artboard? What is its width?

2. Ms. Wang wants to frame her picture with wooden molding.
   a. How much molding would she need to construct a frame around the artboard?
   b. If she decided to frame just the photograph, how much less molding would she need?
   Think of 2 ways to figure out the answer.

3. How should Ms. Wang place the photograph so that it is in the center of the artboard? Describe the steps she might take.

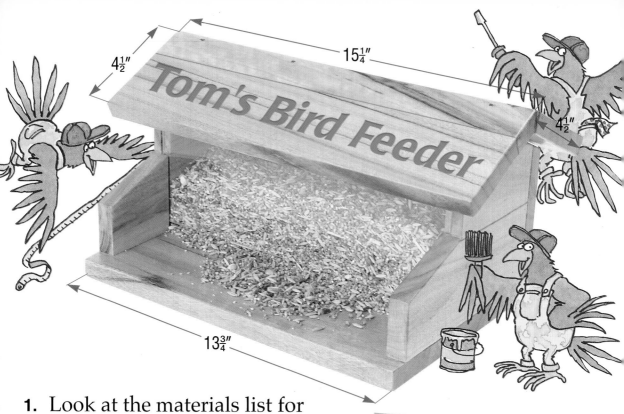

Tom's Bird Feeder

$15\frac{1}{4}''$

$4\frac{1}{2}''$

$4\frac{1}{2}''$

$13\frac{3}{4}''$

1. Look at the materials list for the bird feeder. What is the total length of 3-inch board Tom used to make the roof?

2. What length of board did Tom use to make the complete feeder?

3. If Tom had started with a 12-foot piece of board, how much would he have left?

4. Tom started with $1\frac{1}{2}$ pounds of nails. How many feeders could that amount of nails make?

MATERIALS
(All boards are 3 inches wide.)
Roof: Three $15\frac{1}{4}$ inch boards
Back: Two $13\frac{3}{4}$ inch boards
Left side: One $4\frac{1}{2}$ inch board
One $7\frac{1}{2}$ inch board
Right side: One $4\frac{1}{2}$ inch board
One $7\frac{1}{2}$ inch board
Bottom: Three $13\frac{3}{4}$ inch boards
Front: Plexiglas $4\frac{1}{2}$ inch
by $12\frac{1}{2}$ inch
Other: $\frac{1}{4}$ pound of nails,
2 hinges, varnish, glue

5. Twelve friends each ordered a bird feeder from Tom. Would a 2-foot by 3-foot piece of Plexiglas be enough to make fronts for 12 feeders? How do you know?

Judy and Paulo used pattern blocks to help them add fractions. They used the yellow block as one whole.

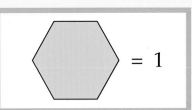
= 1

1. What fraction is represented by:

a.

b.
c.

d.

e.

2. Judy and Paulo used different methods to add $\frac{1}{2}$ and $\frac{1}{6}$.

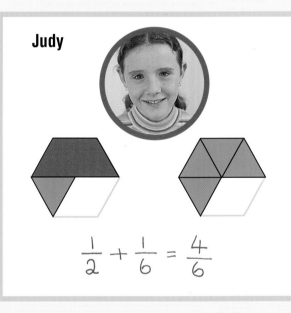

Judy

$$\frac{1}{2} + \frac{1}{6} = \frac{4}{6}$$

Paulo

$$\frac{1}{2} + \frac{1}{6} = \frac{2}{3}$$

Are Judy and Paulo's answers equivalent? How do you know?

3. Use pattern blocks to show these addition problems and the solutions.

a. $\frac{1}{3} + \frac{1}{6}$ b. $\frac{2}{3} + \frac{1}{6}$ c. $\frac{1}{2} + \frac{1}{3}$ d. $\frac{4}{3} + \frac{1}{6}$

Which answers could be written and shown a different way?

4. Use blocks to help you create and solve your own fraction addition problems. Then challenge a partner to solve them.

This catalog page shows how you can buy bags of bows from the Buttons 'n' Bows company.

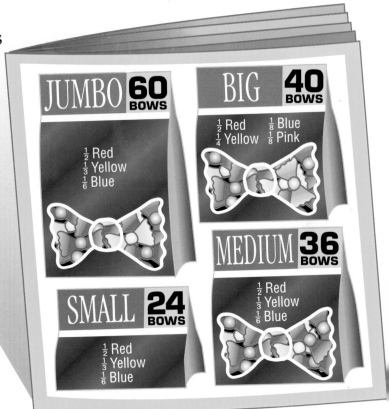

JUMBO **60 BOWS**
½ Red
⅓ Yellow
⅙ Blue

BIG **40 BOWS**
½ Red   ⅛ Blue
¼ Yellow ⅛ Pink

MEDIUM **36 BOWS**
½ Red
⅓ Yellow
⅙ Blue

SMALL **24 BOWS**
½ Red
⅓ Yellow
⅙ Blue

1. How many yellow bows are in each of the following bags?
   a. a jumbo bag
   b. a medium bag
   c. a small bag

2. Which number of bows is greater?
   a. blue bows in a jumbo bag or yellow bows in a small bag
   b. red bows in a small bag or blue bows in a medium bag
   c. blue bows in a medium bag or pink bows in a big bag

3. Suppose you bought two jumbo bags.
   a. How many yellow bows would you get?
   b. What fraction of the total would be yellow bows?

4. Suppose you bought a jumbo bag and a big bag.
   a. What fraction of the total would be yellow bows?
   b. Would the fraction of red bows in the total be the same as in the jumbo bag? How do you know?

5. Suppose you bought one of each kind of bag.
   a. What fraction of the total would be red bows? How do you know?
   b. Figure out the fraction for each of the other colors.

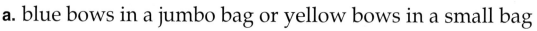

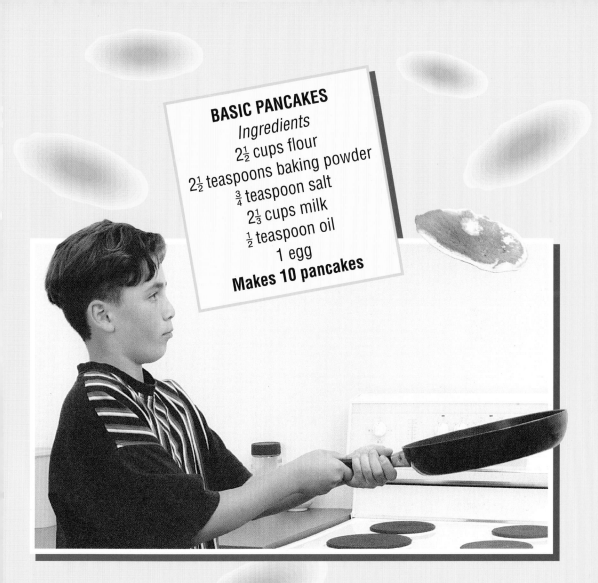

BASIC PANCAKES
Ingredients
$2\frac{1}{2}$ cups flour
$2\frac{1}{2}$ teaspoons baking powder
$\frac{3}{4}$ teaspoon salt
$2\frac{1}{3}$ cups milk
$\frac{1}{2}$ teaspoon oil
1 egg
Makes 10 pancakes

1. Conan plans to make 50 pancakes to raise money.
   a. How much flour does he need? What are some different ways he could figure it out?
   b. What quantity does Conan need of each of the other ingredients. Explain how you decided.

2. Conan has $3\frac{1}{2}$ cups of flour in a bowl.
   How much more does he need for 50 pancakes?

3. What fraction of a dozen eggs is needed for 50 pancakes?

4. Conan estimates that each person uses $\frac{1}{8}$ pint of syrup on pancakes. How many pints will he need for 20 people?

A fifth-grade class learned that the Chagga people used their body measurements to help them plan their houses. Door *heights* were equal to a man's armspan. Door *widths* were equal to the circumference of a man's head.

1. Some students measured the head circumference for each person in a group of 5.
   a. What is the mean circumference for the group?
   b. What is the middle number when you list the circumferences from longest to shortest?
   c. What door width do you think the group would suggest? Why?

Head circumference	
Travis	59 cm
Tamika	56 cm
Joshua	53 cm
Benjamin	54 cm
Derek	55 cm

2. Make your own groups of 5. For your group find:
   a. the mean head circumference
   b. the *median* of the 5 circumferences.

3. Measure your classroom door.
   a. How does the door width compare to the circumference of *your* head?
   b. How does the door height compare to the length of *your* armspan?

A newspaper survey reported the number of advertisements shown by major channels in one week during prime time.

. In each category, estimate what the total advertising time would be if:

a. half the ads lasted one minute and the other half lasted 30 seconds.

b. half the ads lasted one minute, one-fourth lasted 30 seconds, and one-fourth lasted 15 seconds.

4 MAJOR TV CHANNELS
PRIME TIME ADVERTISEMENTS
SEPTEMBER 20–26

CATEGORY	NUMBER
RESTAURANTS/FAST FOOD	136
CARS	104
FOOD AND BEVERAGES	96
DRUG STORES/MEDICINES	88
HOTELS/MOTELS	72
ELECTRONICS	64
TRAVEL	56

. There are 4 major TV channels. Calculate the mean number of ads *per channel* in a week for:

a. cars   **b.** drug stores/medicines   **c.** travel

. If the mean number of toys and games ads shown by the 4 major channels that week was 13.75, what was the *total* number of toys and games ads?

. Calculate the mean number of ads *per day* for each of these. (Use a calculator and round your answers to the nearest hundredth.)

a. restaurants/fast food   **b.** hotels/motels   **c.** electronics

. Suppose prime time is 6:00 p.m. to 10:00 p.m. How could you find the mean number of food and beverage ads *per hour* for the week? Think of some other ways. Then check to be sure that each way gives you the same answer.

Sophie constructed two pie graphs to show how she spent her time on a school day and a weekend day.

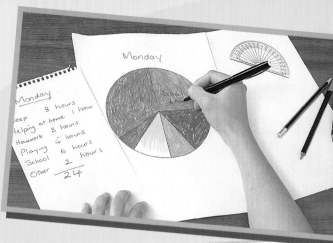

1. On each graph, which activity takes:
   a. the most time?
   b. the least time?

2. Which section of the two graphs has a center angle that is greater than 90 degrees?

3. Which section do you think has a center angle that is exactly 90 degrees? How did you decide?

4. Estimate which sections have a center angle measuring close to:
   a. 60 degrees
   b. 45 degrees
   c. 120 degrees
   d. 30 degrees

5. Use a protractor to check your estimates in Question 4. Explain how you could use fractions to estimate.

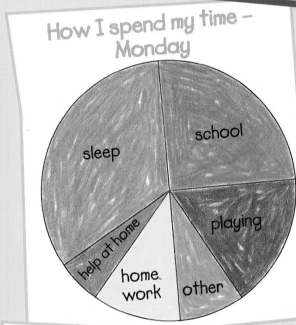

At Dale's Diner, the computer prints out a check when customers finish their meal. Each check records the time and the amount of the sale.

DALE'S DINER
OCTOBER 23 12:21

SOUP	
½ SANDWICH	$1.95
ICE TEA	$3.25
	$1.25
SUB-TOTAL	
TAX	$6.45
TOTAL	.38
	$6.83

CHECK CLOSED: 12:51

1. Look at the check that is pictured.
   a. What is the total amount of the sale?
   b. At what time was the check closed?

Dale's computer graphed sales during the busiest time of the day.

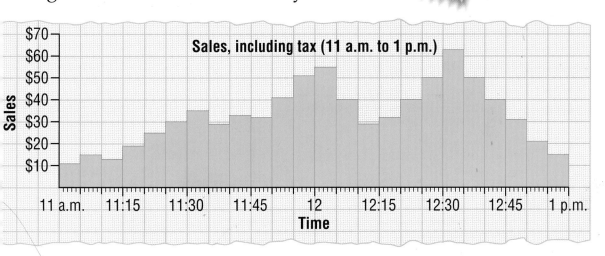

Sales, including tax (11 a.m. to 1 p.m.)

2. Look at the graph. What information is given along:
   a. the vertical axis?   b. the horizontal axis?

3. Estimate the amount of sales, including tax, between:
   a. 11:20 a.m. and 11:25 a.m.   b. 11:55 a.m. and 12:05 p.m.

4. Look at the 3 highest sales amounts shown on the graph.
   a. Between which times were the checks closed for those sales?
   b. Why do you think the sales were highest at those times?

5. How might Dale use the graph?

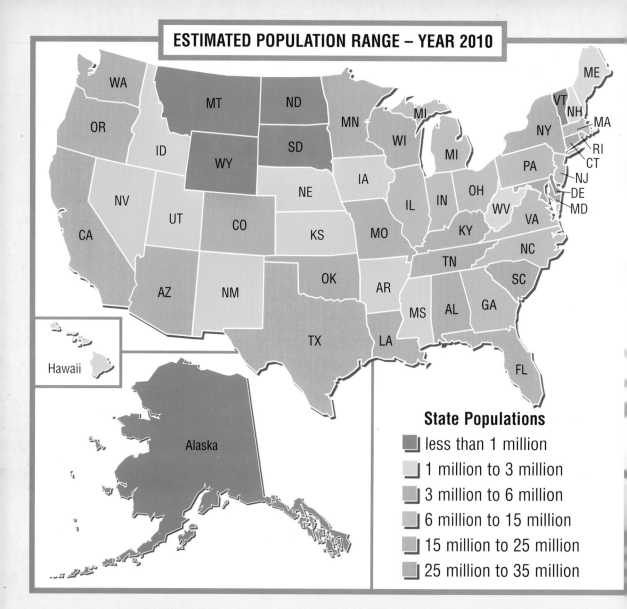

ESTIMATED POPULATION RANGE – YEAR 2010

Hawaii

Alaska

State Populations
- less than 1 million
- 1 million to 3 million
- 3 million to 6 million
- 6 million to 15 million
- 15 million to 25 million
- 25 million to 35 million

1. Look at the map of estimated populations for the year 2010.
   a. In which category does your state belong?
   b. Do you think that your state fits the high, middle, or low end of its category?

2. What other states are in the same category as your state?

3. What color would you use for states with these populations?
   a. 15,032,000   b. 501,625   c. 5,989,765   d. 19,975,019

4. List all the states that share a border with your state. Write the population *range* for each.

. Could a state that is in a *different* category than your state have a population of a similar size? Explain your answer.

. In the year 2010, what is the *lowest* population predicted for:
a. your state? **b.** each of your neighboring states?
How do you know?

. List all the states that will have a population of between 6 million and 15 million in the year 2010. For those states:
a. What is the *total minimum* population predicted?
b. What is the *total maximum* population predicted?

. Work with a partner.
a. Predict what the *total* population of the United States might be in the year 2010.
b. Compare your prediction to the most recent United States population figure. Do you think your prediction for the year 2010 is reasonable? Why or why not?

The Sunshine State's population grew nearly one million in 10 years

Mega City population increased about one-half million in same period

1. What words in the headlines tell you that the population figures are not exact?

2. What are some other ways you could write $\frac{1}{2}$ million?

3. What could the exact population increase be for:
   a. the Sunshine State?　　**b.** Mega City?
   Give 4 different population increase figures for each.

4. Write population figures to match these.
   Give 4 population figures for each.
   a. almost $1\frac{1}{4}$ million　　**b.** nearly $7\frac{1}{2}$ million
   c. over $\frac{1}{4}$ million　　**d.** about $2\frac{3}{4}$ million
   e. between $1\frac{1}{2}$ million and $1\frac{3}{4}$ million

5. Write a newspaper headline for each of these.
   Use fractions in your headlines.
   a. 1,550,000　　**b.** 2,222,222　　**c.** 7,767,340　　**d.** 1,850,000

1. Mike plans to buy 6 bags of
   porcelain beads and 6 bags of wooden beads.
   a. How many beads will he buy altogether?
   Find more than one way to figure out the answer.
   b. What is the total cost of the beads Mike plans to buy?
   How did you figure it out?

2. Angela plans to buy 8 bags of wooden beads and 8 bags
   of glass beads.
   This is how she figured out how
   many beads she would get.

   $$(18 + 12) \times 8 = 240$$

   a. Describe the steps she used.
   b. What different method could she have used?

3. Use Angela's method to calculate the number of beads in:
   a. 7 bags of porcelain beads plus 7 bags of ceramic beads
   b. 6 bags of glass beads plus 6 bags of metal beads.
   Figure out the total cost for each purchase.

4. Figure out the number of beads and the total cost for:
   a. 6 bags of ceramic beads plus 6 bags of wooden beads
   b. 8 bags of pottery beads plus 8 bags of glass beads
   c. 5 bags of ceramic beads plus 5 bags of metal beads.
   Explain in writing how you found each answer.

Mr. Ng needs to order cards to fill this greeting card display.

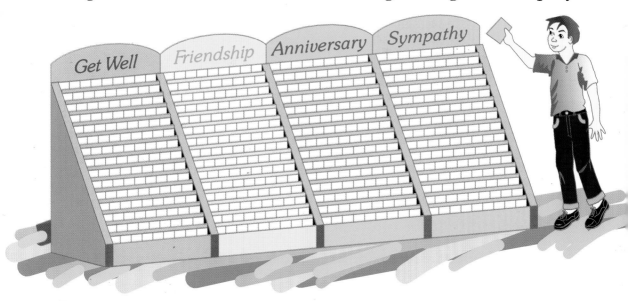

1. Look at the display.
   a. How many rows and columns are in *each section*?
   b. How many rows and columns are in the *whole display*?

2. How many spaces are in the whole display? How do you know?

3. Solve these problems for Mr. Ng.
   a. Suppose he puts 3 cards in each space.
   How many cards will he need to order to fill the display?
   b. Suppose he pays 40 cents for each card.
   How much will it cost to put 3 cards in each space?
   Explain how you solved each problem.

4. Suppose Mr. Ng decides to use one of the sections for more expensive cards. If each card costs 79 cents, how much will it cost him to put 2 cards in each space?

5. How many spaces are in each of these displays?
   a. 14 rows and 27 columns   **b.** 15 rows and 45 columns
   c. 16 rows and 54 columns   **d.** 16 rows and 72 columns

Some teachers at Fairview School recorded the time they spend driving to and from school each day.

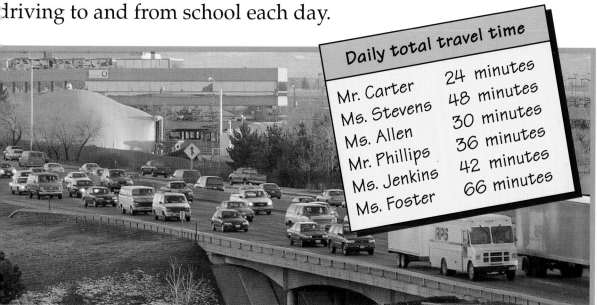

Daily total travel time

Mr. Carter	24 minutes
Ms. Stevens	48 minutes
Ms. Allen	30 minutes
Mr. Phillips	36 minutes
Ms. Jenkins	42 minutes
Ms. Foster	66 minutes

. Give the total weekly travel time for each teacher:
   a. in minutes   **b.** in hours

. Suppose the teachers average a travel speed of 45 miles per hour.
   a. What distance does each teacher travel to and from school in one week?
   b. How did you figure out the distances?

. Suppose the cost for operating a car is 65 cents per mile.
   a. Use a calculator to find how much it costs each teacher to travel to school each week.
   b. How did you figure out the costs?

. Work in a group to make a chart showing each teacher's travel time, distance, and cost.

. Use the information in your chart to estimate the time, distance, and cost for each teacher for:
   a. 4 weeks   **b.** 12 weeks   **c.** one school year (36 weeks)

Shaika and Renzo made a simple pattern block design. Then they used a pair of hinged mirrors to make their design look complete.

1. Look at the complete design that Shaika and Renzo made.
   a. Describe the simple design.
   b. How many times can you see the simple design in the complete design?

2. Look at the 2 complete designs below.
   a. Point to the simple design.
   b. How many times can you see the simple design in each complete design?

mirror   mirror

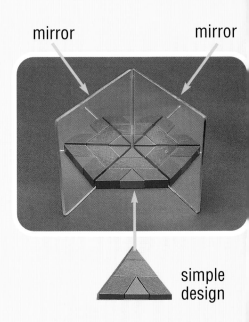

simple design

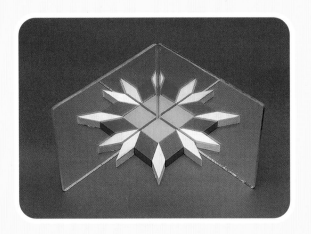

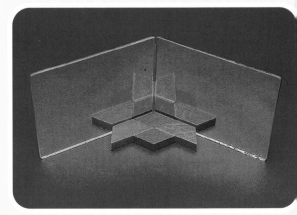

3. Use pattern blocks and a pair of mirrors to make your own complete design. For each complete design you make:
   a. Count the number of times you can see the simple design.
   b. Describe what you notice about the angle of the mirrors.
   c. What did you discover about the angle of the mirrors and the number of times you could see the simple design?

SYMMETRICAL LINE DESIGNS

Anna likes to construct designs that show symmetry.

1. What steps did Anna use to construct the designs on this page?

2. What is the size of each small angle at the center of Anna's design? How did you find out?

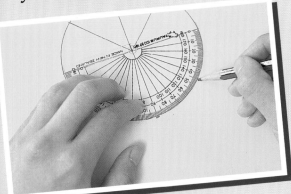

3. What kind of symmetry do you see:
   a. in the Step 3 design?
   b. in the Step 4 design?

4. Using the same steps with a different number of spokes, make your own symmetrical design. Figure out the size of the center angles.

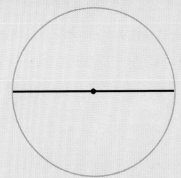

Step 1: Draw a circle and 2 spokes.

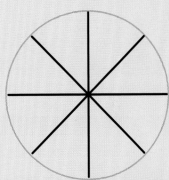

Step 2: Use a protractor to help draw 6 more spokes equally spaced.

Step 3: Erase the circle and draw a square at the end of each spoke.

Step 4: Add another square at the end of each spoke.

Oscar drew a map of his paper route. He wrote on the map the number of customers who lived on each section of the route.

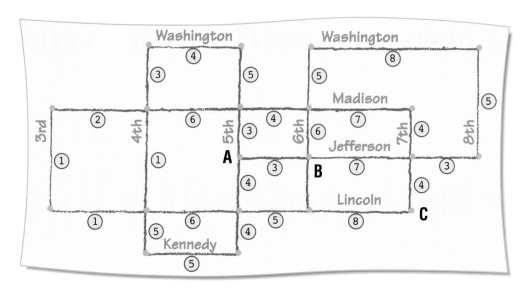

1. Look at the section on Madison between 6th and 7th Streets. How many customers live there?

2. Could Oscar walk his paper route without going over any section twice if he started at:
   a. Point A?   **b.** Point B?   **c.** Point C?

3. Use your findings from Question 2 to locate another possible starting corner. Are there any other possible starting corners? Where would it be best for Oscar to live?

4. Look at the 2 possible starting corners.
   How many sections meet at each of these corners?

5. Look at all the other corners.
   a. How many sections meet at each of these corners?
   b. How are these corners different from the starting corners?

6. Suppose Oscar stopped delivering papers to streets with only one or two customers. Could he still walk his paper route without going over any section twice?

DECADES OF THE 20th CENTURY

1. How many years are there in:
   a. one decade?
   b. one century?

2. Find two events on the timeline that are:
   a. about one decade apart
   b. about 3 decades apart
   c. about half a century apart.

3. How many years before you were born did a person first walk on the moon?

4. From the timeline or your own research, find an important event that happened in the fourth decade of the 20th Century.

5. What is the date of:
   a. the last day of the 20th Century?
   b. the first day of the 21st Century?

6. America celebrated the bicentennial of the Declaration of Independence in 1976. In which year was the Declaration of Independence signed?

7. Make a timeline of the important events in *your* state during the 20th Century.

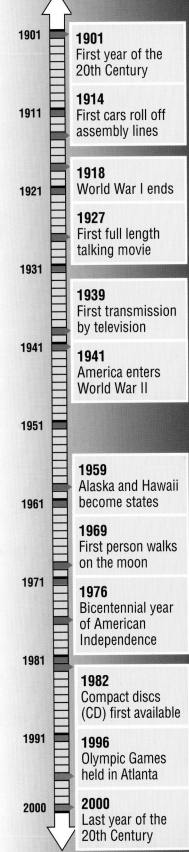

1901 First year of the 20th Century

1914 First cars roll off assembly lines

1918 World War I ends

1927 First full length talking movie

1939 First transmission by television

1941 America enters World War II

1959 Alaska and Hawaii become states

1969 First person walks on the moon

1976 Bicentennial year of American Independence

1982 Compact discs (CD) first available

1996 Olympic Games held in Atlanta

2000 Last year of the 20th Century

1. What do you notice about the times shown on the map?

2. How many time zones are there across the 48 states?

3. What time zone are you in? What are some cities in your time zone?

4. What time is it in Los Angeles when it is:
   a. 6 o'clock in New York?   b. 11 o'clock in New York?
   c. 6 o'clock in Denver?   d. 2 o'clock in Houston?

5. Imagine that you are in Miami and your grandmother is in San Francisco. During what hours would it be best to call her to wish her a happy birthday?

6. At 6 a.m. in Denver, Philip is getting out of bed. What do you think people might be doing in each of the other time zones?

This timetable shows departure and arrival times
for some non-stop flights out of New York City.
The arrival times are local time, not New York time.

New York to Chicago			New York to Denver			New York to Los Angeles		
Flight	Depart	Arrive	Flight	Depart	Arrive	Flight	Depart	Arrive
EW 37	8:25 a.m.	9:54 a.m.	EW 125	8:10 a.m.	10:39 a.m.	EW 615	8:00 a.m.	11:04 a.m.
EW 39	10:00 a.m.	11:20 a.m.	EW 127	10:00 a.m.	12:10 p.m.	EW 617	10:00 a.m.	1:08 a.m.
EW 41	1:00 p.m.	2:21 p.m.	EW 129	12:30 p.m.	2:37 p.m.	EW 619	12:00 noon	2:59 p.m.
EW 43	4:30 p.m.	5:55 p.m.	EW 131	5:00 p.m.	7:12 p.m.	EW 621	4:00 p.m.	7:04 p.m.
EW 45	9:00 p.m.	10:15 p.m.	EW 133	6:30 p.m.	8:52 p.m.	EW 623	9:00 p.m.	12:05 a.m.

1. When it is 10:00 a.m. in New York, what time is it in:
   a. Chicago?   b. Denver?   c. Los Angeles?

2. Figure out the length (in hours and minutes) of:
   a. the 10:00 a.m. flight to Chicago
   b. the 10:00 a.m. flight to Denver
   c. the 10:00 a.m. flight to Los Angeles.
   Remember to allow for different time zones.

3. Figure out the length (in hours and minutes) for flight:
   a. EW 129 to Denver   b. EW 621 to Los Angeles
   c. EW 43 to Chicago   d. EW 45 to Chicago.

4. Which flight from New York to Denver takes the longest time?
   How did you figure out your answer?

5. Why do you think times for non-stop flights between the same
   two cities are not always the same length?

1. Which piece of cheese should Carole buy?

2. Does the amount of juice shown on the label agree with the claim in the ad?

3. The odometer on the car shows miles and tenths of a mile. How will the driver know when he has traveled $1\frac{3}{4}$ miles?

At a Weather Station, instruments are checked every 6 hours.
The rain gauge is emptied at 9 a.m. each day.

. Look at the rain gauge
readings in the chart below.
   a. How much rain fell in the
   24-hour period?
   b. How much rain fell in each
   6-hour period?
   c. How much more
   rain fell in the second
   12-hour period than
   the first 12-hour period?
   Explain how you figured each answer out.

A rain gauge measures rainfall in inches.

A mercury barometer measures air pressure in inches.

Rain gauge readings for 24 hours				
9 a.m.	3 p.m.	9 p.m.	3 a.m.	9 a.m.
0 inches	0.6 inches	0.9 inches	1.7 inches	2.38 inches

. Look at the barometer readings in the chart below.
   a. Describe how the mercury fell in the
   24-hour period.
   b. How far did the mercury fall in each
   6-hour period?

Barometer readings for 24 hours				
9 a.m.	3 p.m.	9 p.m.	3 a.m.	9 a.m.
31.25 inches	30.85 inches	30.42 inches	29.65 inches	29.4 inches

. The average air pressure at sea level is 29.92 inches.
How close to the average air pressure was each
barometer reading?

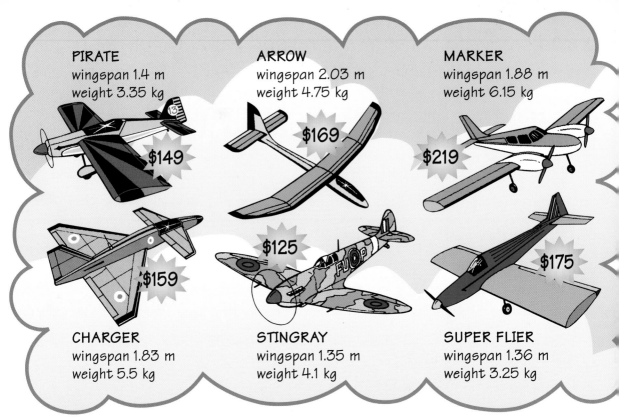

PIRATE
wingspan 1.4 m
weight 3.35 kg
$149

ARROW
wingspan 2.03 m
weight 4.75 kg
$169

MARKER
wingspan 1.88 m
weight 6.15 kg
$219

CHARGER
wingspan 1.83 m
weight 5.5 kg
$159

STINGRAY
wingspan 1.35 m
weight 4.1 kg
$125

SUPER FLIER
wingspan 1.36 m
weight 3.25 kg
$175

1. Look at the advertisement. Which model has:
    a. the longest wingspan?　　　　**b.** the greatest weight?

2. How much longer or shorter is each wingspan than:
    a. 1 meter?　　　　　　　　　　　**b.** 2 meters?

3. What is the difference between the wingspans of:
    a. Marker and Charger?　　　　**b.** Marker and Stingray?
    c. Marker and Pirate?　　　　　**d.** Arrow and Charger?
    e. Arrow and Pirate?　　　　　　**f.** Arrow and Super Flier?

4. What is the difference between the weights of:
    a. Arrow and Super Flier?　　　**b.** Arrow and Pirate?
    c. Arrow and Charger?　　　　　**d.** Marker and Stingray?

5. One of the largest model gliders ever built is the Nemere.
    It has a wingspan of 3.333 meters.
    What is the difference between the wingspan of Nemere and:
    a. Arrow?　　　　**b.** Charger?　　　　**c.** Pirate?

Matt and Lim used one-inch square grid paper to cut out rectangles. They used the rectangles as **bases** to build box shapes.

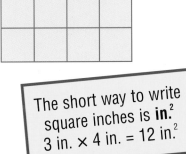

1. What are the **dimensions** of each rectangle?

2. What is the **area** of each rectangle?

The short way to write square inches is **in.**^{2}
3 in. × 4 in. = 12 in.^{2}

These are the box shapes Matt and Lim built on each base.

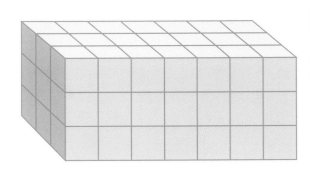

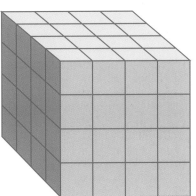

3. What is the **height** of each shape?

4. Matt and Lim each wrote a rule for finding the volume of a box shape.

The short way to write cubic inches is **in.**^{3}
3 in. × 4 in. × 6 in. = 72 in.^{3}

Volume = Area of base × h   Volume = l × w × h

   a. Use both rules to find the **volume** of each box shape above.
   b. Describe how the two rules are the same.

5. Calculate the volume of each of these shapes.
   a. 5 in. × 13 in. × 6 in.   **b.** 6 in. × 16 in. × 12 in.

1. Look at the centimeter cube.
   a. What is the length of each side?
   b. What is the cube's volume?
   c. How many milliliters of water would fill a one-cubic-centimeter container?

2. Look at a thousands cube.
   a. Give its dimensions in:
      • decimeters   • centimeters
   b. Give its volume in:
      • cubic decimeters
      • cubic centimeters
   c. How much water does a cubic-decimeter container hold? Give your answer in:
      • liters   • milliliters

Paulo's class built this cubic-meter container.

3. Look at the cubic-meter container.
   a. Give its 3 dimensions in:
      • decimeters
      • centimeters
   b. Give its volume in:
      • cubic decimeters
      • cubic centimeters
      What did you notice?
   c. How much water would it hold? Give your answer in:
      • liters   • milliliters

Some students made a list of objects that weighed about 1 kilogram. Then they made a list of objects that weighed about 1 gram.

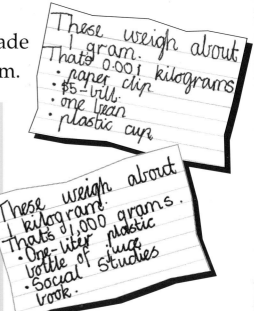

These weigh about 1 gram. That's 0.001 kilograms
• paper clip
• $5 bill
• one bean
• plastic cup

These weigh about 1 kilogram. That's 1,000 grams.
• One-liter plastic bottle of juice
• Social Studies book.

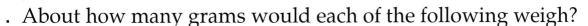

1. About how many grams would each of the following weigh?
   a. 3 bottles of juice
   b. 2 social studies books
   c. 1,000 $5 bills
   d. 1,500 beans
   e. 500 paper clips
   f. 10 plastic cups

2. Give your answers to Question 1 in kilograms.

3. Ann carried 2 water bottles on a hike. One bottle could hold 1 liter. The other could hold 1.5 liters. How many kilograms of water could Ann carry?

4. Containers for the Spring Water Cooler hold 18.9 liters. Each empty container weighs 0.5 of a kilogram.
   a. Estimate the weight of 10 full containers.
   b. Suppose a truck can carry 10,000 kilograms. About how many containers of Spring Water is that?

One liter of water weighs one kilogram

Nicki and Bill collected water from a dripping faucet.
Each half hour, they measured the amount of water.
This is the graph they made.

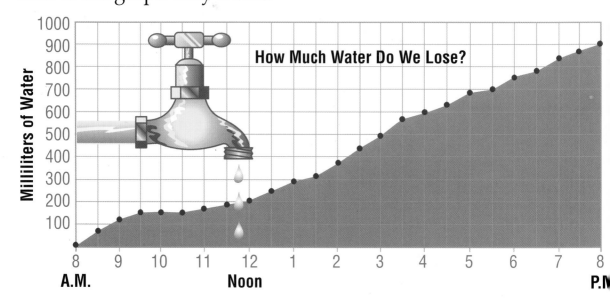

1. Look at the graph.
   a. For how many hours did Nicki and Bill collect water?
   b. How much water did the faucet drip during that time?

2. How much water had the faucet dripped by:
   a. 11:30 a.m.?   b. 3:30 p.m.?   c. 6:30 p.m.?

3. How much water did the faucet drip between:
   a. 11:30 a.m. and 12:30 p.m.?   b. 6:30 p.m. and 7:30 p.m.?
   c. 9:30 a.m. and 10:30 a.m.?

4. What was the average number of milliliters
   of water dripped per hour for the 12-hour period?

5. About how much water do you think the faucet would
   drip in 24 hours?

6. If the faucet continued to drip the same amount each
   day, how many liters of water would be wasted in:
   a. 2 days?   b. one week?   c. 4 weeks?   d. one year?

RAVENOUS
2 mini pizzas
per person

HARRY'S
MINI PIZZA
SPECIALS

STARVING
$1\frac{1}{2}$ mini pizzas
per person

HUNGRY
$1\frac{1}{4}$ mini pizzas
per person

Harry specializes in mini pizzas.
Look at his "per person" specials.

. Four friends each ordered Harry's "Ravenous" special.
How many mini pizzas did each person get?
How many mini pizzas in all did the friends order?

. How many mini pizzas would Harry serve for the following
orders of the "Starving" special?
a. 2 orders   **b.** 3 orders   **c.** 5 orders

. How many pizzas would 6 friends get:
a. if each person orders the "Starving" special?
b. if each person orders the "Hungry" special?
Explain how you figured out each answer.

. Near closing time Harry had $2\frac{1}{2}$ mini pizzas left over.
If Harry ate $\frac{1}{4}$ of the leftover pizzas, how much pizza
did he eat?

. Work in a group. Make up some problems that involve
multiplying fractions.

GINGERBREAD

Ingredients:
$\frac{1}{4}$ pound butter, softened
$\frac{1}{3}$ cup granulated sugar
$\frac{3}{4}$ cup brown sugar
2 teaspoons ground ginger
2 large eggs, beaten
$3\frac{1}{3}$ cups of flour
$\frac{1}{4}$ teaspoon salt
$\frac{1}{2}$ teaspoon cinnamon
$\frac{1}{4}$ teaspoon allspice
$\frac{3}{4}$ teaspoon baking soda
$\frac{1}{4}$ cup hot water

Cream butter, sugar, brown sugar, and ginger; add eggs; mix well. Add flour, salt, and spices, and baking soda dissolved in hot water. Knead, roll out $\frac{1}{4}$ inch thick, cut into shapes, bake 15-20 min. at 350°F.

Dale plans to make 6 batches of gingerbread to sell at the school bake sale.

1. How much of each of the following ingredients will Dale nee
   a. cinnamon   **b.** butter   **c.** brown sugar

2. Dale measured his granulated sugar and flour to check if he had enough for 6 batches of gingerbread.
   a. He found that he had $2\frac{1}{3}$ cups of sugar. Was this enough to make 6 batches of the recipe? Explain how you know.
   b. Dale had 19 cups of flour. Did he need more flour than this to make 6 batches? How do you know?

3. Suppose Dale decided to make more gingerbread. Make a cha to show the amount of each ingredient needed for:
   a. $\frac{1}{2}$ batch   **b.** $5\frac{1}{2}$ batches.

Derrick and Kate wanted to find a fraction of a fraction. These are the steps they used to find $\frac{1}{3}$ of $\frac{2}{5}$.

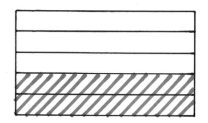   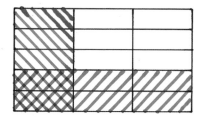

Step 1: Divide the rectangle into **fifths**. Cross-hatch $\frac{2}{5}$ of the rectangle.

Step 2: Divide the rectangle into **thirds**. Cross-hatch $\frac{1}{3}$. Use the cross-hatching to help you find the answer to $\frac{1}{3}$ of $\frac{2}{5}$.

1. Look at the steps Derrick and Kate used.
   a. How do you think they figured out the fraction that is cross-hatched in two directions?
   b. Why do you think they separated the rectangle in the opposite direction when showing the thirds?
   c. What is $\frac{1}{3}$ of $\frac{2}{5}$?

2. Suppose the picture drawn for Step 1 looked like this: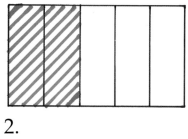
   a. Describe how Derrick and Kate would have done Step 2.
   b. Would their answer have been the same? Explain how you know.

3. Derrick's mom bought a sheet cake. How could she figure out how to cut:
   a. $\frac{1}{4}$ of $\frac{1}{2}$ of the sheet cake?
   b. $\frac{1}{2}$ of $\frac{1}{3}$ of the sheet cake?

4. Find the answers to these:
   a. $\frac{1}{2}$ of $\frac{3}{8}$ b. $\frac{1}{3}$ of $\frac{3}{5}$
   c. $\frac{1}{2}$ of $\frac{3}{5}$ d. $\frac{1}{4}$ of $\frac{3}{4}$

This is the final leg of a 400-meter relay. Each leg of the race is 100 meters.

Team	First Leg	Second Leg	Third Leg	Fourth Leg
Gazelles	13.9 sec.	14.4 sec.	13.58 sec.	13.44 sec.
Leopards	14.06 sec.	14.1 sec.	13.72 sec.	13.8 sec.
Cheetahs	13.6 sec.	13.95 sec.	13.97 sec.	14.2 sec.

1. For each relay leg, which team had the fastest time? How did you determine this?

2. Which team won the relay?

3. Did any of the teams break the school record?

400-meter relay
School Record
55.4 seconds

4. What was the difference in the total times of the winning team and the team that came in third?

5. For each team:
   a. calculate the average (mean) time for running one leg of the race
   b. find which runner's time was closest to the average time for his team.

6. The Tigers team ran a mean time of 13.94 seconds. What was the Tigers' total time? How did you figure it out?

SAM'S MUSIC CENTER
Best buys in town on audiotapes!

30-minute tapes	60-minute tapes	90-minute tapes
6-pack $4.50	6-pack $5.40	6-pack $6.30
4-pack $3.08	4-pack $3.80	4-pack $4.36
3-pack $2.49	3-pack $2.94	3-pack $3.39
single $0.89	single $0.99	single $1.19

1. Calculate the cost per tape in:
   a. one 4-pack of 30-minute tapes
   b. one 4-pack of 90-minute tapes
   c. one 3-pack of 30-minute tapes
   d. one 3-pack of 90-minute tapes.
   How did you figure out the costs?

2. Use your answers to Question 1 to predict the cost per tape in:
   a. one 6-pack of 30-minute tapes
   b. one 6-pack of 90-minute tapes.
   How did you make your predictions?

SPECIAL OFFER!

Up to $20 worth of tapes **FREE** when you purchase a Super Sound cassette player.

3. Calculate the cost per tape in each pack of 60-minute tapes.

4. Suppose Sam wanted to sell tapes in 8-packs.
   Which of these prices do you think would be reasonable?
   a. $5.76 for 30-minute tapes   b. $7.60 for 60-minute tapes
   c. $8.32 for 90-minute tapes

5. Suppose you bought the Super Sound cassette player.
   What combination of tape packs would you choose? Why?

Buy Fresh Fruit in Bulk!
Bargain buys. Low, low prices!

240 pears

360 peaches

480 apples

420 oranges

1. Suppose 4 families buy fruit in bulk and share it. How many of each kind of fruit will each family get if they buy:

   a. pears? **b.** peaches? **c.** apples? **d.** oranges?

2. The Valdez family store Bargain Buys in their cold storage room. They eat 40 pieces of fruit per week. How long will a Bargain Buy last if they buy:

   a. pears? **b.** peaches? **c.** apples? **d.** oranges?

   Did you use the answers from Question 1 to help you?

3. Divide the number of pieces of fruit in each Bargain Buy:

   a. by 3 (for 3 families) **b.** by 30 (for 30 children in a class).

   Copy and complete the chart.

Divide by	Pears	Peaches	Apples	Oranges
3				
30				

4. Divide the number of pieces of fruit in each Bargain Buy by 60. How did you figure out each answer? What pattern did you see?

Three San Francisco families went on vacation. They chose different destinations and used different kinds of transport.

San Francisco to New York
Distance: 2,585 miles
Travel time: 5 hours

San Francisco to Los Angeles
Distance: 376 miles
Travel time: 8 hours

San Francisco to Reno
Distance: 252 miles
Travel time: 7 hours

. Calculate the average distance each vehicle travels per hour. What word do we use for this rate?

. What unit do we use to measure speed?

. Figure out the average speed for each of these car trips. Give your answers in miles per hour.
   a. *Distance:* 282 miles, *Time:* 6 hours
   b. *Distance:* 329 miles, *Time:* 7 hours
   c. *Distance:* 496 miles, *Time:* 8 hours

. Solve each of these problems.
   a. A car traveled for 6 hours at an average speed of 55 m.p.h. What distance did it travel?
   b. Mario drove for 220 miles at an average speed of 50 m.p.h. About how many hours did his journey take?

. Create some problems that involve distance, time, and speed.

Salina surveyed her class to find the most popular sports. She made this chart and pie graph to show the results.

Favorite Sport	Number of People
Basketball	12
Football	6
Baseball	5
Swimming	3
Tennis	3
Soccer	1
Total	30

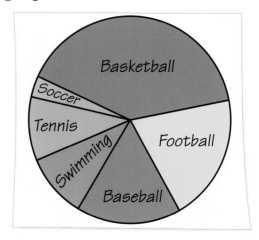

1. Look at the number of people whose favorite sport is basketball. Compare this to the number who prefer:
   a. football   b. swimming   c. soccer.

2. What number would make the following sentence true?
   The number of people who chose basketball is ____ times the number who chose tennis.

3. Work with a partner. Copy the following sentence 3 times. Fill the gaps to make each sentence true.
   The number of people who chose _____ is ____ times the number who chose _____.

4. Write a ratio to show the number of people who prefer:
   a. basketball to swimming
   b. baseball to football
   c. tennis to swimming.

   > The ratio of people who prefer basketball to tennis can be written as
   > 12:3
   > This is read as "12 to 3."

5. What sports do you think Salina compared to get the following ratios?
   a. 12:6   b. 6:1   c. 3:5   d. 1:3

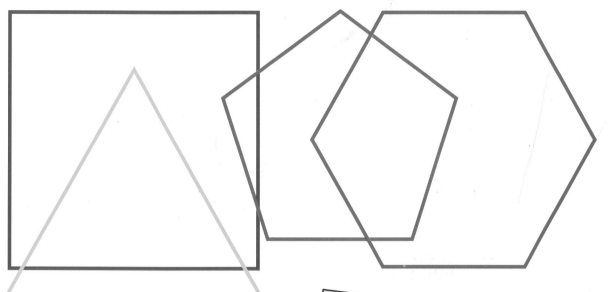

1. Look at each shape above.
   a. In what ways are these shapes the same?
   b. In which shape is each angle equal to 90 degrees?
   c. Which shape has acute angles that are equal?

Shape	Number of angles	Size of each angle	Sum of the angles
Equilateral triangle	3	60°	180°
Square			
Regular pentagon			
Regular hexagon			

2. Copy and complete the chart. Use a protractor to measure any angles you do not know.

3. What patterns do you see in the chart?
   a. How does the size of each angle change for each shape?
   b. How does the sum of the angles change for each shape?

4. Predict the sum of the angles in a regular polygon that has:
   a. 8 sides   **b.** 10 sides   **c.** 15 sides.

5. Use your answers to Question 4 to figure out the size of each angle in a regular polygon that has:
   a. 8 sides   **b.** 10 sides   **c.** 15 sides.

Some students measured the circumference and diameter of circular objects to see if they could find a pattern. Here are the steps they followed.

Step 1: Place a streamer around the circumference of the object. Mark "**C**" where the 2 ends meet.

Step 2: Stretch the streamer across the diameter. Carefully mark "**d**" for diameter.

Step 3: Extend the length of the circumference across the diameter. Estimate how many times the diameter would fit along the circumference.

Step 4: Use a measuring tape and a calculator to figure out how many times the diameter would fit along the circumference.

1. These are the measurements they recorded for the pipe planter.
   a. Estimate to find about how many times greater the circumference is than the diameter.
   b. Use your calculator to find the answer.

$C = 55$ in.
$d = 17\frac{1}{2}$ in.

After they had measured several objects,
the students made a chart of their findings.

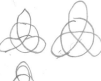

C = 55 in.
d = 17.5 in.

pipe planter

C = 130 in.
d = 41.4 in.

large table

C = 69 in.
d = 22 in.

bicycle wheel

C = 75 in.
d = 24 in.

small table

C = 31.25 in.
d = 10 in.

circular tray

2. Look at the chart. What do you notice when you estimate to compare each circumference to its diameter?

3. For each circle in the chart, divide its circumference by its diameter. What did you discover?

4. Read the Mathnet, and then solve these problems.

   a. A wheel has a diameter of 2 feet. What is its circumference?

   b. If you draw a circle with a radius of 6 inches, what is the circumference? Describe the steps you used.

MATHNET

Even in ancient times, people knew that when they divided the circumference of a circle by its diameter, the answer was always **a little more than 3**. For thousands of years, mathematicians tried to find an exact fraction. This proved to be impossible.

In 1706, William Jones, an Englishman, suggested that the exact value should be called "pi" (π), a letter of the Greek alphabet. Today we write:

$$C \div d = \pi.$$
π is a **little more than** 3.14.

Nerida used a compass and a ruler
to draw a symmetrical design.
Look at the steps she used.

1. Suppose the radius of the
   larger circle is 4 inches.
   What is the diameter of each circle?

2. Calculate the circumference of:
   a. the larger circle   **b.** the smaller circle.
   What do you notice about
   the 2 circumferences?

3. Calculate the circumference of circles
   with these diameters:
   a. 8 inches   **b.** 16 inches   **c.** 32 inches.
   What do you notice?

4. Calculate the circumference of circles
   with these diameters:
   a. 10 inches   **b.** 11 inches   **c.** 12 inches.
   How does the circumference of a
   circle change when the diameter
   increases by one inch?

5. Copy Steps 1 and 2.
   a. Measure each angle of the triangle.
   What did you discover?
   b. Draw lines as shown in Step 3,
   and measure each center angle.
   What did you notice?

6. Color your design. Try to
   make it symmetrical.

Step 1: Draw a
circle. Then draw
a circle with the
same center but
twice the radius.

Step 2: Draw strai
lines that just touc
the inside circle to
make a triangle.

Step 3: Draw 3 lin
from the center to
corners of the tria

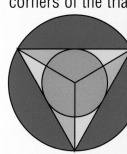

Step 4: Color
the design.

Kate and Derrick helped Mr. Brown and Ms. Green to plan their garden plot.

. Mr. Brown had $\frac{1}{3}$ of the plot and wanted to plant $\frac{3}{4}$ of it with beans. So Kate and Derrick drew this diagram to find what fraction of the plot to plant with beans. How much of the **total plot** should be planted with beans?

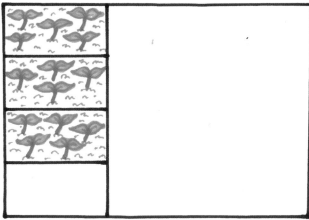

Mr. Brown showed a quicker way to find a fraction of a fraction.

$$\frac{3}{4} \times \frac{1}{3} = \frac{3}{12}$$

That's $\frac{1}{4}$.

. Ms. Green has $\frac{2}{3}$ of the plot. She wants to plant $\frac{3}{8}$ of her share with lettuces.
  a. Find how much of the **total plot** to plant with lettuces.
  b. Describe what happens when you multiply a fraction by a fraction.

. Mr. Brown wants to plant $\frac{1}{8}$ of his $\frac{1}{3}$ plot with radishes. What fraction of the **total plot** should be planted with radishes?

. Ms. Green wanted to plant $\frac{1}{4}$ of her $\frac{2}{3}$ plot with carrots. How much of the **total plot** should be planted with carrots?

. Find the answers to these:
  a. $\frac{1}{2} \times \frac{3}{4}$ **b.** $\frac{3}{4} \times \frac{1}{4}$ **c.** $\frac{1}{3} \times 1\frac{1}{4}$ **d.** $\frac{3}{5} \times 2\frac{1}{4}$
  Remember to give each fraction in its simplest form. Explain your answers.

Several fifth-grade students were adding and subtracting fractions.

1. Todd thought $\frac{1}{2} + \frac{1}{3}$ might be $\frac{2}{5}$. Do you think he was right? Why or why not?

2. Todd decided to use fraction strips to help him find $\frac{1}{2} + \frac{1}{3}$.

1 whole				
$\frac{1}{2}$			$\frac{1}{3}$	
$\frac{1}{6}$	$\frac{1}{6}$	$\frac{1}{6}$	$\frac{1}{6}$	$\frac{1}{6}$

   a. Why did Todd use the $\frac{1}{6}$ strips?

   b. What does $\frac{1}{2} + \frac{1}{3}$ equal?

3. The fraction strips below show $\frac{1}{2} + \frac{3}{10}$.

   a. What fraction strips could Todd use in the next row?

   b. Give the sum of $\frac{1}{2}$ and $\frac{3}{10}$ in two ways.

1 whole			
$\frac{1}{2}$	$\frac{1}{10}$	$\frac{1}{10}$	$\frac{1}{10}$

4. Describe how Todd could use fraction strips to help figure out $\frac{1}{2} + \frac{2}{5}$.

5. Find the following sums in their simplest form. Use your fraction strips to help you.

   a. $\frac{1}{4} + \frac{3}{8}$ b. $\frac{1}{4} + \frac{1}{3}$ c. $\frac{1}{2} + \frac{2}{3}$ d. $\frac{3}{4} + \frac{2}{3}$

6. Zia thought of a method of using fraction strips to show subtraction. This is how she figured out that $\frac{4}{5} - \frac{1}{2} = \frac{3}{10}$. Explain the steps in Zia's method.

1 whole			
$\frac{1}{5}$	$\frac{1}{5}$	$\frac{1}{5}$	$\frac{1}{5}$
$\frac{1}{10}$ $\frac{1}{10}$ $\frac{1}{10}$		$\frac{1}{2}$	

7. Use Zia's method to figure out:

   a. $\frac{5}{6} - \frac{2}{3}$ b. $\frac{3}{4} - \frac{2}{3}$ c. $\frac{3}{4} - \frac{1}{3}$ d. $\frac{2}{3} - \frac{1}{4}$

   Give each answer in its simplest form.

Pam's
APPLE PIE
85 cents per
large piece

Pam's
BLUEBERRY PIE
75 cents per
medium piece

1. Look at the two pies. What fraction of a pie is:
   a. one large piece? **b.** one medium piece?
   c. 4 large pieces? **d.** 6 medium pieces?

2. Figure out the total amount of pie in each of these orders.
   Express each fraction in its simplest form.
   a. 3 large pieces and
   4 medium pieces
   b. 2 large pieces and
   2 medium pieces
   c. 5 large pieces and
   4 medium pieces
   d. 4 large pieces and
   5 medium pieces

3. Pam sold a total of $\frac{2}{3}$ of a pie to one customer.
   Find two different combinations of pieces that the customer
   could have bought. (You can draw a picture to help you.)

4. There were $6\frac{3}{8}$ blueberry pies left. Then $2\frac{3}{4}$ blueberry pies were
   sold. What quantity of blueberry pie was left?

5. There were $2\frac{1}{2}$ apple pies left on the shelf. Then Ms. Randle
   bought $\frac{1}{3}$ of all the apple pie that was left.
   a. What is $\frac{1}{3}$ of $2\frac{1}{2}$ apple pies?
   b. How much apple pie was left?
   Check to make sure that your answers make sense.

6. Which do you think is the better buy, a medium-sized piece
   or a large-sized piece? How did you decide?

1. About how much snow must fall to provide the same amount of water as:
   a. 3 inches of rain?
   b. 4.5 inches of rain?
   c. 0.4 inches of rain?

2. About how much rain must fall to provide the same amount of water as:
   a. 20 inches of snow?
   b. 35 inches of snow?
   c. 7 inches of snow?

3. Look at the high rainfall figures on the chart. If the precipitation had fallen as snow, how much snow would there have been in:
   a. San Antonio?   b. Bismarck?
   c. Springfield?   d. Jacksonville?
   How did you figure out each answer?

4. Look at each of the snowfall figures on the chart. If the precipitation had occurred on a hot summer's day, how much rain would have fallen on each city? How do you know?

5. One of the wettest places in the world is Mount Wai-ále-ále in Hawaii. Suppose the mean daily rainfall for one month was 2.54 inches. Predict how much rain would fall:
   a. in 10 days   b. in 15 days.

10 inches of snow contains about the same amount of water as one inch of rain.

PRECIPITATION EXTREMES

Some high 24-hour readings for U.S. cities

SNOW

March 13, 1995
Albany, New York
26.6 inches of snow

March 13, 1995
Syracuse, New York
35.6 inches of snow

RAIN

May 5, 1995
San Antonio, Texas
6.26 inches

July 15, 1995
Bismarck, North Dakota
5.27 inches

September 24, 1995
Springfield, Missouri
6.27 inches

November 30, 1995
Jacksonville, Florida
4.05 inches

Ms. Miller made this quilt from **2-inch** squares. Before she began, she created a grid for the design.

. Think about the size of each square. Use this information to figure out the quilt's:
  a. dimensions
  b. perimeter
  c. area.

. Suppose Ms. Miller made a 20-square by 20-square quilt using **one-inch** squares. Figure out the quilt's:
  a. dimensions
  b. perimeter
  c. area.

. Suppose Ms. Miller had made a 20-square by 20-square quilt from **larger** squares. Look at the chart below and figure out the new measurements.

Size of squares used to make quilt	1″ by 1″	2″ by 2″	3″ by 3″	4″ by 4″	5″ by 5″	6″ by 6″
Dimensions of quilt	20″ by 20″	40″ by 40″				
Perimeter of quilt	80 in.	160 in.				
Area of quilt	400 in.^{2}	1600 in.^{2}				

4. What patterns do you see in the measurements?

Ivan, a landscape gardener, always draws plans to help him figure out area.

1. Look at his plan for a patio.
   a. What unit would Ivan use to measure the area?
   b. How could Ivan "break up" the plan to make it easier to calculate the total area?
   c. What is the total area of the patio?

2. Look at the plan for the pool and paved surround.
   a. How does Ivan's figuring help determine the area to be paved?
   b. What is the area to be paved?

3. Use Ivan's method to help you calculate the area of each plan below.

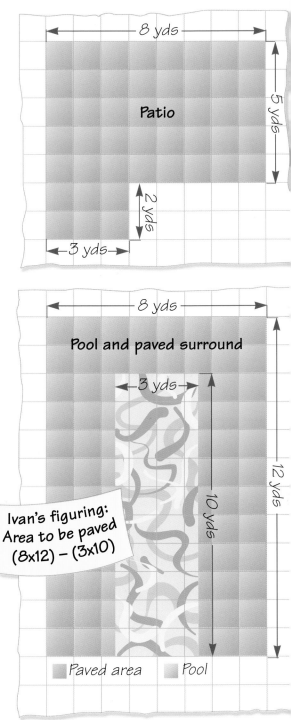

8 yds

Patio

5 yds

2 yds

3 yds

8 yds

Pool and paved surround

3 yds

12 yds

10 yds

Ivan's figuring:
Area to be paved
(8x12) – (3x10)

Paved area   Pool

25 yds

12 yds

5 yds

4 yds

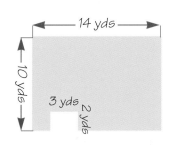

14 yds

10 yds

3 yds   2 yds

Max drew a parallelogram on centimeter grid paper. Then he cut it up so he could find its area.

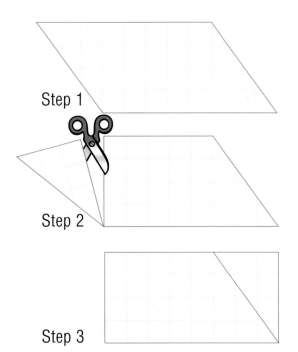

Step 1

Step 2

Step 3

1. Look at Step 1.
   a. Why do you think the shape is called a parallelogram?
   b. What is the height of the parallelogram? What is the length of its base?

2. Look at Steps 2 and 3.
   a. What shape did Max make?
   b. What is the height and the length of the rectangle's base?
   c. How did rearranging the parallelogram help Max to find its area?
   d. What is the area of the parallelogram?

3. Some other students drew parallelograms on centimeter grid paper. For each parallelogram below, give:
   a. its dimensions
   b. its area.
   Explain how you figured out the area.

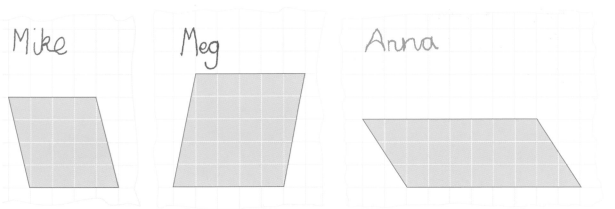

Mike

Meg

Anna

4. Draw some parallelograms on centimeter grid paper. Figure out the area of each parallelogram.

Mandy, Carla, Javier, and Tomás wanted to make pennants for their soccer club. They needed to find the area of triangles, so they began by drawing triangles on a one-inch grid.

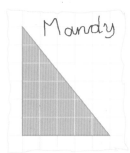

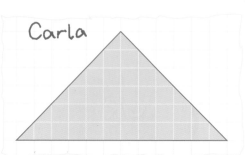

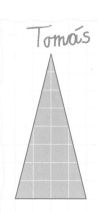

Mandy   Carla   Javier   Tomás

1. For each triangle Mandy and her friends drew:
   a. find the length of its base and its height
   b. explain how you could calculate the area.

   Mandy and her friends each wrote a rule.

   Area = one half of $(b \times h)$
   Mandy

   Area $= \dfrac{(b \times h)}{2}$
   Javier

   Area $= (b \times h) \div 2$
   Carla

   Area $= \frac{1}{2} \times b \times h$
   Tomás

2. Explain how to use the four rules to find the area of Mandy's triangle. What did you discover?

These are the pennants Mandy and her friends plan to make.

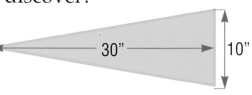

30"   10"

18"   6"

3. Use any of the rules to calculate the areas of the 2 pennants.

4. How many pennants do you think could be made from a square yard of material if:
   a. the larger pennants were made?
   b. the smaller pennants were made?

Katy and Ben were trying to figure out the **area** of a circle.

1. Ben drew a circle on grid paper.
   a. Why do you think he did this?
   b. Estimate the area of Ben's circle. How did you make your estimate?

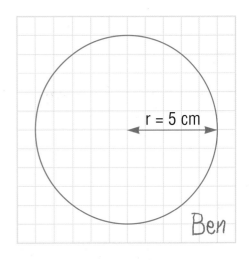

2. Katy drew a regular decagon around her circle.
   a. How do you think the area of the **circle** would compare to the area of the **decagon**?
   b. How do you think Katy could figure out the area of the decagon?

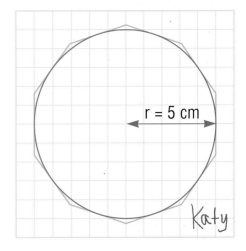

3. Katy divided the decagon into 10 equal triangles. Then she cut out one triangle.
   a. How could Katy figure out the area of the triangle?
   b. What is the height of the triangle? How do you know?
   c. Measure the length of the base of the triangle. Find the area of:
      • the triangle
      • the decagon
   d. Estimate the area of the circle.

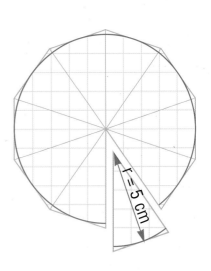

Mr. McDonald recorded the length of the best standing jump each of his students made. Then the class made a stem-and-leaf plot to show the data.

Length of standing jumps

Centimeters

164, 173, 182, 157, 171,
146, 158, 149, 155, 182,
166, 172, 166, 158, 176,
158, 152, 186, 191, 145,
163, 177, 188, 174, 190

Stem-and-Leaf Plot

Length of standing jumps

Stem	Leaves
	Centimeters
14	5 6 9
15	2 5 7 8 8 8
16	3 4 6 6
17	1 2 3 4 6 7
18	2 2 6 8
19	0 1

1. List the jump lengths in order from shortest to longest. Find:
   a. the median   **b.** the mode.

2. Compare your list with the stem-and-leaf plot.
   Can you see how the plot was made? What does the 14 in the stem column represent?

3. How would you find the number of students who jumped 166 cm:
   a. using the data on the clipboard?
   b. using the stem-and-leaf plot?

4. Look at the stem-and-leaf plot.
   a. How many students jumped more than 175 cm?
   b. How many students jumped between 145 cm and 175 cm?
   Explain how the stem-and-leaf plot made it easier to answer the questions.

5. Measure the best standing jump for each member of your class Then make a stem-and-leaf plot to display the data.

The 3 spinners were made by different groups – the Tigers, Lions, and Rams.

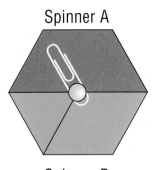

Spinner A

. Look at the way each spinner is colored.
   a. For which spinner is red the **most** likely outcome?
   b. For which spinner is green the **least** likely outcome?
   c. For each spinner, describe the likelihood of getting blue as an outcome.

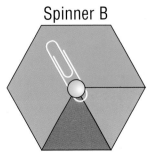

Spinner B

. Tom spun one of the spinners. The outcome was green. Which spinner did Tom most likely use?

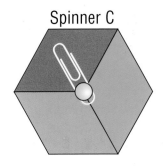

Spinner C

. Each group graphed the outcomes of 30 spins of their spinner. Which group do you think made spinner: A?   B?   C?

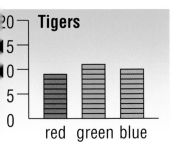

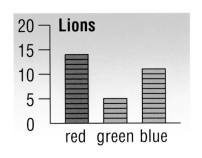

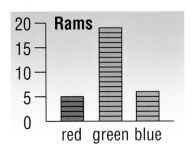

. Three groups used regular hexagons to make spinners. For each graph below, draw what its spinner might look like.

a.

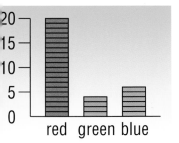

b.

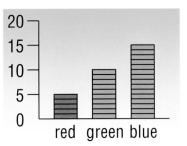

c.

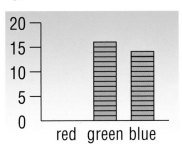

Josh and Leah wanted to find out which color was the most popular for the whole school. First they used their class as a sample.

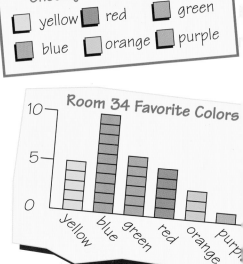

Check your favorite color

☐ yellow ■ red ☐ green

☐ blue ☐ orange ■ purple

1. How many students in Room 34 answered the questionnaire?

2. Look at the graph. What fraction of the class chose blue? Express the fraction in simplest form.

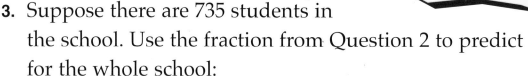

Room 34 Favorite Colors

3. Suppose there are 735 students in the school. Use the fraction from Question 2 to predict for the whole school:
   a. the *fraction* of students likely to choose blue
   b. the *number* of students likely to choose blue.

4. Use the sample to predict the number of students in the whole school who would pick as their favorite color:
   a. green   b. red   c. yellow   d. orange   e. purple.

5. Here are the results of a pet survey in Room 35.
   a. How many students were in the sample?
   b. What fraction of the sample chose each pet?
   c. Predict how many students in the whole school would choose each pet.

Room 35 Favorite Pets

8 dog   6 cat

3 guinea pig   1 fish

4 bird   2 rabbit

6. Conduct a "favorite color" or "favorite pet" survey, or make up some questions of your own. Use your class as a sample and predict the results for the whole school. Report your findings with a data display to the class.

A hobby group made this layout for their model cars. They used the coordinates on the grid to give directions for moving cars from one point to another.

(2,9) means across 2, up 9.

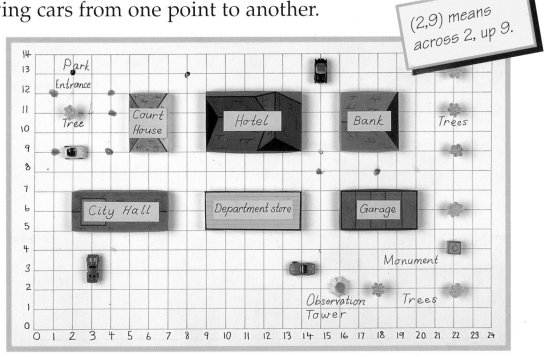

1. What is located at each of these points?
   a. (2,11)   b. (15,13)   c. (22,2)   d. (16,7)

2. Which coordinates give the location of:
   a. the yellow car?   b. the monument?
   c. the observation tower?

3. Suppose you are moving the red car. Follow these instructions.
   Go to (3,4), turn right… go to (8,4), turn left…
   go to (8,13), turn left…   go to (2,13), turn right.
   Where is the red car now?

4. Write instructions for each of these journeys.
   a. Move the blue car to the park entrance.
   b. Park the black car between the bank and the garage.
   c. Move the yellow car in a square around the tree at (2,11).

Rick and Ella made toothpick patterns. Then they plotted points to show the number of squares they made and the number of toothpicks they used.

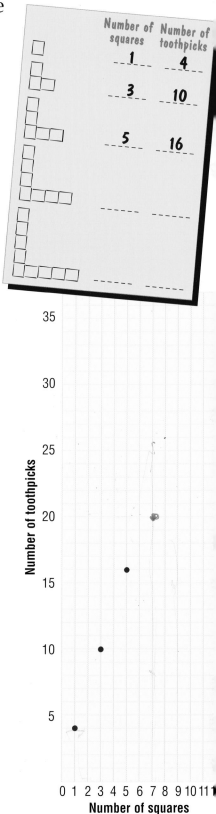

Number of squares	Number of toothpicks
1	4
3	10
5	16

1. Look at the chart that Rick and Ella made. Find the number of squares and the number of toothpicks in:
   a. the fourth shape on the chart
   b. the fifth shape on the chart
   c. the next shape in the pattern.

2. Look at the graph.
   a. Give the coordinates of each of the 3 points.
   b. Give the coordinates of the points for the fourth, fifth, and sixth shapes.

3. Put a ruler along the 3 points on the graph.
   a. What did you notice?
   b. Why doesn't it make sense to draw a straight line to connect the points?
   c. How could you use the ruler to help you figure out the coordinates of the next points in the pattern?

4. Give the coordinates of:
   a. the seventh point in the pattern
   b. some other points in the pattern that would not fit on the graph.

Number of toothpicks

35

30

25

20

15

10

5

0 1 2 3 4 5 6 7 8 9 10 11 1
Number of squares

Tim plotted the point (11,16) to show his age and the age of his sister, Cory. Then he plotted points to show their ages at their next 3 birthdays. He drew a straight line through the points.

1. Look at the graph. Give the coordinates of each point Tim plotted.

2. For each ordered number pair:
   a. what information does the first number give?
   b. what information does the second number give?
   Who is older, Tim or Cory? How do you know?

3. Did it make sense for Tim to join the points with a line? Explain your answers.

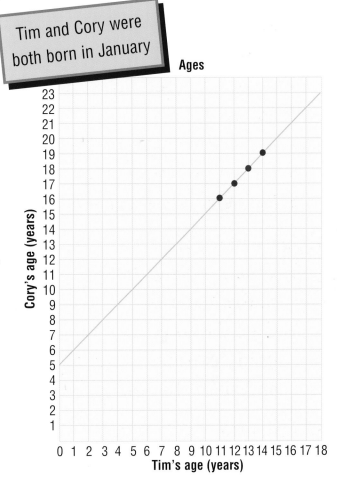

Tim and Cory were both born in January

Ages

Cory's age (years)

Tim's age (years)

For Questions 4 to 7, give your answers to the closest whole year.

4. How old was Cory:
   a. when Tim was 8 years old?
   b. when Tim was born?

5. How old will Tim be when Cory is 21?

6. How old will Cory be when Tim is 21? How do you know?

7. What rule could you use to figure out:
   a. Cory's age if you know Tim's age?
   b. Tim's age if you know Cory's age?

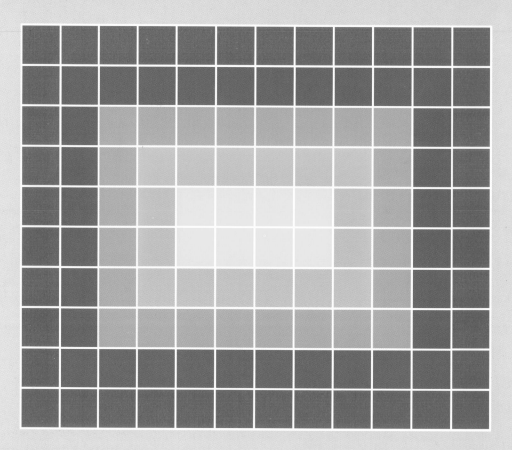

1. Look at the tile design. Describe how the tiles
   have been arranged.

2. How many tiles are:
   a. yellow?   **b.** orange?   **c.** green?   **d.** blue?   **e.** red?
   Describe how the number pattern grows.

3. How many brown tiles would you need to put around
   the edge of the design? Explain how you can use
   the number pattern to find the answer.

4. How many tiles are in the rectangle made by:
   a. the yellow and the orange tiles?
   b. the yellow, the orange, and the green tiles?
   c. the yellow, the orange, the green, and the blue tiles?
   d. all the tiles?
   What pattern can you find in the answers?

Terry used a grid to enlarge a drawing.

. Look at the 2 boat hulls.

  a. Working clockwise,
record the coordinates
of the four corners of
the big hull in a chart
like this.

Coordinates of hull corners

small boat	(2,1)	(2,2)	(7,2)	(6,1)
big boat	(6,3)			

  b. What do you notice
about the numbers
in the table?

  c. How did Terry make her enlargement?

. Suppose each square on the grid is one square inch.

  a. What is the area of the hull on:
- the small boat?
- the big boat?

  b. What is the area of the sail on:
- the small boat?
- the big boat?

What did you discover?

. Draw a bigger rocket ship.
Make each dimension
4 times greater.

  a. Explain what you did.

  b. Find the area of
your rocket ship.

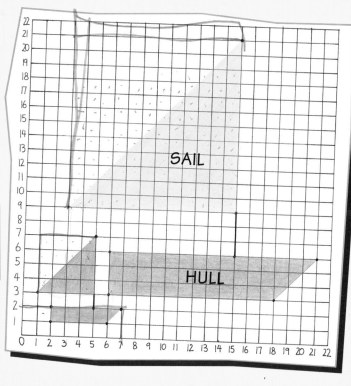

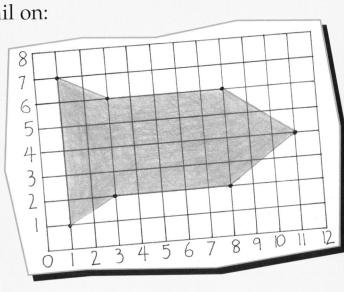

Some students made shape patterns on a geoboard. Then they copied the patterns onto dot paper.

1. Look at these shapes the students drew.

   a. What do you think they did to make their pattern?

   b. How does each new shape in the pattern change?

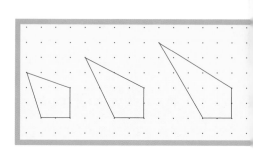

2. The students thought the area of each new shape was greater than the shape just before it. What do you think?

3. The students drew dotted lines to change each shape into a square. How do you think they were able to figure out the area of an irregular polygon?

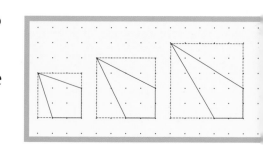

4. For each shape above:

   a. write the area of the square

   b. find the area of the 2 triangles

   c. subtract the area of the triangles from the area of the square. (Give all measurements in square units.)

5. Look at these shapes.

   a. Copy the shapes onto dot paper and draw the next 2 shapes in the pattern.

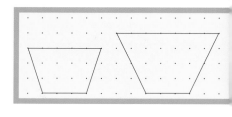

   b. Draw a rectangle around each shape to help you find its area. Explain how the area of the shape increases each time.

Mr. Kasahara showed the class "solid" shapes called *regular polyhedra*.

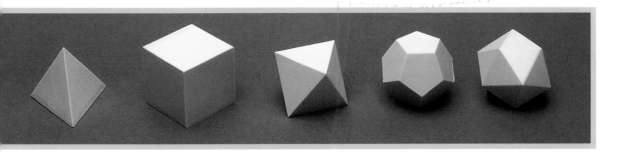

1. Look at each solid shape.
   a. What do you notice about the surfaces?
   b. What shape is each surface?
   Why do you think these solid shapes are called regular polyhedra?

2. The class made a chart to show the number of surfaces, vertices, and edges in each of the regular polyhedra.
   a. What do you notice about the numbers in the chart?
   b. Try to find a rule that tells the relationship between the number of surfaces, vertices, and edges.

	Tetrahedron	Hexahedron	Octahedron	Dodecahedron	Icosahedron
Surfaces	4	6	8	12	20
Vertices	4	8	6	20	12
Edges	6	12	12	30	30

3. Find some other solid shapes that have only flat surfaces.
   a. For each shape, count the number of surfaces, vertices, and edges.
   b. Does the rule you found in Question 2 work for each shape?

4. Investigate shapes that have curved surfaces, such as a cone, cylinder, and sphere. Does the rule work for these shapes?

Analyzing solid shapes   **79**

Ben took apart some boxes to investigate how they were made.

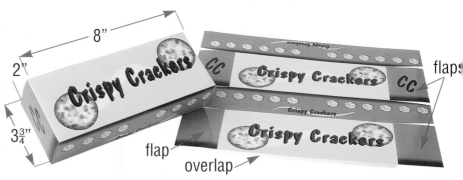

1. How do you think the cardboard was cut, folded, and glued to make the Crispy Crackers box?

2. What are the dimensions of the smallest rectangle of cardboard that could have been used to make the Crispy Crackers box? (Allow $\frac{1}{2}$ in. for the overlap .)

3. How many Crispy Crackers boxes do you think could be made from one square yard of cardboard?

4. How many square yards of cardboard do you think would be needed to make 10,000 boxes?

5. Estimate the dimensions of the smallest rectangle of cardboard that could be used to make each of the following boxes. (Allow $\frac{1}{2}$ in. for any overlap.)

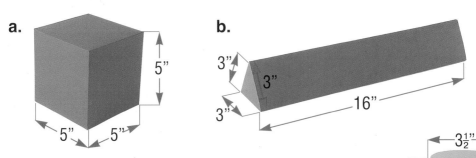

a.

b.

6. Estimate the dimensions of the smallest rectangle of cardboard needed to make:
   a. the side of the cylinder
   b. the lid and base of the cylinder.
   (Remember to allow for the joins.)

ON SALE

BETTER THAN ½ PRICE

46 OZ UNSWEETENED Orange Juice

46 OZ UNSWEETENED Orange Juice

UNSWEETENED Orange Juice

Regular price $1.69 per can
Now 2 for $1.49

. Look at the advertisement for orange juice.

   a. The ad claims that the sale price is "better than ½ price."
   Is this correct? How do you know?

   b. For 2 cans, how much cheaper is the sale price
   than the regular price?

. Suppose you buy juice at the "on sale" price.

   a. How much do you pay for these purchases?
   - 4 cans   • 6 cans   • 10 cans   • 12 cans

   b. For each purchase, how much less would you pay for the
   "on sale" cans than buying them at the regular price?

. Suppose the store pays $6.96 for a box of 12 cans of juice.
  Calculate the store's profit on each box if the cans are sold:

   a. at the "on sale" price   **b.** at the regular price.

. Suppose a restaurant buys boxes of cans at the "on sale"
  price and sells the juice at 75 cents for a 6-ounce glass.

   a. How many ounces of orange juice are there in 12 cans?

   b. How many glasses could be poured from a box of cans?

   c. How much profit would be made on each box of juice?
   Explain how you figured out your answers.

The Baxter family run the Power Puzzle Company.
This spreadsheet shows a summary of the company's
sales and expenses for a 4-week period.

	Sales and expenses – March						
Week ending	Sales	Cost of goods sold	Wages	Taxes	Rent and utilities	Postage	Other
Mar.7	$2789.21	$1368.20	$445.20		$900.00	$62.30	$24.59
Mar.14	$2195.42	$1285.20	$660.70		$203.56	$47.50	
Mar.21	$2382.73		$660.70			$96.48	$70.89
Mar.28	$2530.56		$895.30	$1120.16		$104.35	
Total	$9897.92	$2653.40	$2661.90	$1120.16	$1103.56	$310.63	$95.48

1. Look at the column headings on the spreadsheet.
   a. Which column shows **sales**?
   b. Which columns show **expenses**?
   c. Calculate the total expenses for the 4-week period.

2. How would you find out whether the Power Puzzle
   Company made a **profit** or a **loss** over the 4-week period?
   a. What was the profit (or loss)?
   b. About what fraction of the total sales was the profit (or loss)

3. Estimate answers to each of the following questions.
   a. What fraction of the **sales** was the **cost of goods** sold?
   b. What fraction of the **total expenses** were **wages**?
   c. What fraction of the **total expenses** were **rent and utilities**?

4. Estimate the following for one year:
   a. sales   b. total expenses   c. profit.

5. How do you think the Baxters would be able to use their
   monthly spreadsheets to run their company efficiently?

Darren and Kate help the Baxters. They use postal scales to weigh the puzzles and figure out postage costs.

PARCEL POST SERVICE								
lbs	Zone 1	Zone 2	Zone 3	Zone 4	Zone 5	Zone 6	Zone 7	Zone 8
1-2	2.56	2.63	2.79	2.87	2.95	2.95	2.95	2.95
2-3	2.63	2.76	3.00	3.34	3.68	3.95	3.95	3.95
3-4	2.71	2.87	3.20	3.78	4.68	4.95	4.95	4.95
4-5	2.77	2.97	3.38	4.10	5.19	5.56	5.95	5.95
5-6	2.84	3.07	3.55	4.39	5.67	6.90	7.75	7.95
6-7	2.90	3.16	3.71	4.67	6.11	7.51	9.15	9.75
7-8	2.96	3.26	3.85	4.91	6.53	8.08	9.94	11.55
8-9	3.01	3.33	3.99	5.16	6.92	8.62	10.65	12.95
9-10	3.07	3.42	4.12	5.38	7.29	9.12	11.31	14.00
10-11	3.12	3.49	4.25	5.59	7.63	9.59	11.93	15.05
11-12	3.17	3.57	4.37	5.79	7.96	10.03	12.52	16.10
12-13	3.23	3.64	4.47	5.98	8.26	10.45	13.07	17.15
13-14	3.27	3.71	4.59	6.16	8.55	10.84	13.59	18.20
14-15	3.32	3.77	4.69	6.34	8.82	11.22	14.08	19.25
15-16	3.37	3.83	4.79	6.50	9.09	11.58	14.55	20.30
16-17	3.41	3.90	4.88	6.66	9.33	11.92	15.00	21.35
17-18	3.45	3.95	4.97	6.81	9.58	12.24	15.42	22.40
18-19	3.49	4.02	5.06	6.95	9.80	12.55	15.83	23.25
19-20	3.54	4.07	5.14	7.08	10.01	12.84	16.21	23.84
20-21	3.57	4.12	5.23	7.21	10.23	13.12	16.59	24.41
21-22	3.61	4.18	5.30	7.34	10.43	13.39	16.94	24.96
22-23	3.65	4.23	5.39	7.47	10.62	13.66	17.28	25.47
23-24	3.69	4.27	5.46	7.58	10.80	13.90	17.60	25.97
24-25	3.73	4.32	5.53	7.70	10.98	14.14	17.91	26.45

. Look at the chart. Describe how Darren and Kate would figure out the cost of mailing a parcel.

. Use the chart to find the cost of mailing:
   a. a 3 lb 2 oz package to Zone 4
   b. a 9 lb 5 oz package to Zone 6.

. Figure out the cost of mailing each of the following orders. (For each order, add 4 oz for the weight of packing materials used.)

   a. 3 puzzles each weighing 2 lb 12 oz to a customer in Zone 6.
   b. 2 puzzles that weigh 3 lb 9 oz and 2 lb 4 oz to the same address in Zone 8.

. Look at the costs for Zone 3.
   a. What do you notice about the way in which the cost increases down the column?
   b. Find the cost of sending parcels that weigh 5 lb, 10 lb, and 20 lb. What do you notice?

Non-Stop Flight Times

	CHICAGO	DALLAS	LOS ANGELES	MIAMI	NEW YORK	SALT LAKE CITY	SAN FRANCISCO	SEATTLE
DALLAS	2h,10min							
LOS ANGELES	4h,50min	3h,3min						
MIAMI	3h,10min	2h,35min	5h,22min					
NEW YORK	2h,15min	3h,25min	5h,45min	2h,52min				
SALT LAKE CITY	3h,5min	2h,30min	1h,45min	4h,35min	4h,53min			
SAN FRANCISCO	3h,57min	3h,17min	1h,13min	5h,17min	5h,54min	1h,40min		
SEATTLE	3h,40min	5h,8min	2h,28min	5h,32min	5h,53min	1h,45min	1h,55min	
WASHINGTON	1h,45min	3h,8min	5h,25min	2h,31min	1h,10min	4h,46min	4h,45min	4h,30min

1. Look at the chart. Which flight from New York takes the longest time?

2. How much longer is the flight from Salt Lake City to Miami than the flight from Salt Lake City to Los Angeles?

3. Calculate the difference in flying times for the pairs of flights below. Explain the steps you used.
   a. Chicago to Miami. Chicago to Seattle.
   b. Miami to Los Angeles. Miami to New York.
   c. New York to Washington. New York to San Francisco.

4. How much faster is it to take the direct flight from New York to San Francisco than to fly from New York to Salt Lake City, and then to San Francisco?

5. Plan a trip that has at least 4 different flights. Allow one hour for each stop and calculate the total time the trip will take. (Use a map to help you.)

WALK OR RUN! JOIN THE FUN!
13 MILE HALF-MARATHON
STARTS HERE 8 a.m. SATURDAY

WINNER'S TIME
1. Ishmael 1:27:36

YOUR TIME
72. Tracey 1:39:52

YOUR TIME
227. Dylan 1:48:17

Here are Tracey and Dylan's times for running the half-marathon.

1. The winner's time was 1 hour, 27 minutes, 36 seconds.
   How much longer did it take:
   a. Tracey to finish the race?   **b.** Dylan to finish the race?

2. What was the difference between Tracey and Dylan's times?
   Explain how you figured it out.

3. Angelo was 6 minutes and 35 seconds behind Tracey. How did Angelo's time compare with Dylan's time?

11. Darius   1:31:28
12. Neena   1:31:43
13. Dominic 1:33:18
14. Howard 1:33:27
15. Victor   1:34:09

4. Look at the chart that shows the results for 11th through 15th place.
   a. How does each time compare to the winner's time?
   b. How does each time compare to:
   • Tracey's time?
   • Dylan's time?

Marc experimented with 2 wheels to make designs. He used a small wheel with 45 teeth and a large wheel with 150 teeth.

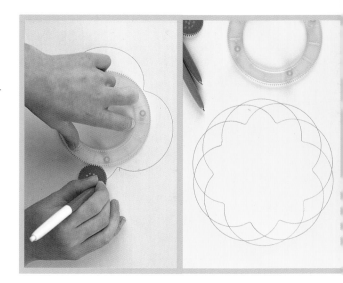

1. When the small wheel turns once, how many teeth on the big wheel does it touch?

2. How many teeth on the big wheel does the small wheel touch when the small wheel turns:

   a. twice?   b. 3 times?   c. 4 times?

3. Suppose the small wheel makes one complete trip around the big wheel.

   a. How many full turns does the small wheel make?

   b. Figure out how many extra teeth the small wheel touches on the big wheel.

   c. Find the quotient and the remainder when 150 is divided by 45. What do you notice?

4. Look at the chart. How did Marc decide what to write in the:

   a. second column?   b. third column?   c. fourth column?

Number of trips made by small wheel around big wheel	Number of teeth touched on big wheel	Number of full turns made by small wheel	Number of extra teeth on big wheel touched by small wheel
1 trip	150	3	15
2 trips	300	6	30
3 trips	450	10	0
4 trips	600	13	15

Peta and Liam sold packages of seeds to help their class raise money. They made this record of their results.

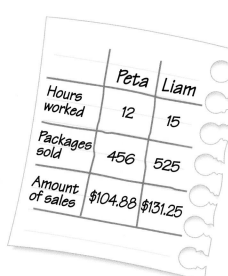

	Peta	Liam
Hours worked	12	15
Packages sold	456	525
Amount of sales	$104.88	$131.25

1. Use a calculator to help you solve these problems.
   a. Who sold the most packages per hour?
   b. Who raised the most money per hour?
      How did you figure out each answer?
   c. Do you think that all the packages of seeds were the same price? Why or why not?

2. Suppose Peta sold seed packages at the same rate for another 3 hours.
   a. How many packages do you predict that she would sell over the 15 hours?
   b. About how much money do you think she would make at the end of the selling period?
   c. How did you figure out each answer?

3. Compare Peta's results for 15 hours with Liam's results for 15 hours. What did you find out?

SUPER SWEATER SALE
Half-price table

$39.90

$58.50

1. Look at the sweaters on the half-price table.
   What is the sale price of a sweater that is marked:
   a. $39.90?   **b.** $58.50?

2. How do you figure out the sale price of sweaters
   on a half-price table?

3. How could you figure out the sale price of sweaters
   on a "one-third off" table?

4. Figure out the sale price of each of these sweaters
   from a "one-third off" table.
   a. a sweater marked $39.90   **b.** a sweater marked $58.50

5. What is the total of each of these sales?
   a. a $36.90 sweater and a $48.90 sweater from the
      half-price table
   b. a $48.90 sweater and a $45.90 sweater from the
      "one-third off" table
   How did you figure out each answer?

6. Copy and complete the chart below.

Marked price	$37.80	$57.60	$65.20	$75.80
One-half off marked price				
One-fourth off marked price				

Ms. Jones showed this photo of high school students. She challenged the class to write different sentences about the number of students with brown hair.

Every other student has brown hair. — Noel

Fifty out of every hundred students have brown hair — Josh

50 percent of students have brown hair. — Paulo

1. Read Noel's sentence. If she is right, what fraction of the students have brown hair?

2. Do Noel and Josh agree? Why or why not?

3. Look at Paulo's sentence. What do you think 50 percent means?

> The word "percent" comes from the Latin "per centum" meaning "by the hundred."

4. Suppose one out of every 4 students rides the bus to school.
   a. How many students out of every hundred ride the bus?
   b. How would you write the answer as a percentage?

5. Suppose 10 percent of students walk to school. What fraction of the students is this? How do you know?

6. Copy the chart.
   a. Write each percentage as a common fraction. (You can use answers from Questions 3, 4, and 5 to help.)

percentage	common fraction	decimal fraction
50%		
25%		
10%		

   b. Write each common fraction as a decimal.
   c. Explain how you figured out what fractions to write.

Georgia put gumballs in different-sized jars. For each jar, she counted the gumballs and then made a pie graph to show the percentage of each flavor.

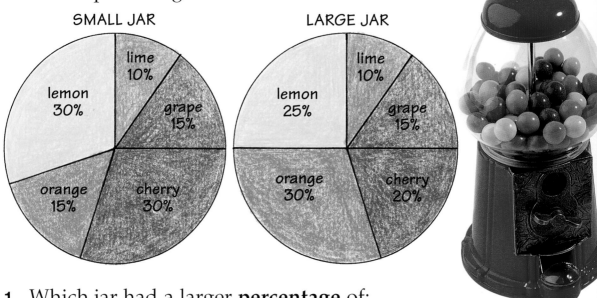

SMALL JAR
LARGE JAR

1. Which jar had a larger **percentage** of:
   a. cherry gumballs? **b.** orange gumballs?

2. Can you tell which jar had a larger **number** of cherry gumballs? Why or why not?

Suppose there were 100 gumballs in the small jar and 160 gumballs in the large jar.

3. For each jar, **estimate** the number of gumballs that were:
   a. lemon   **b.** lime   **c.** grape.
   Explain how you made your estimates.

4. Which jar do you think contained the most cherry gumballs? How could you find out?

5. You know that 10% of 160 is 16. Use this to figure out:
   a. 20% of 160   **b.** 30% of 160   **c.** 40% of 160.

6. If the gumballs in the two jars were mixed together, about what percentage of the total number would be grape?

1. Look at the advertisement for the discount sale.
   a. How are percentages used in the advertisement?
   b. What different discounts are being advertised?
   c. What are some other ways used to show discounts?

2. What fraction would you use to figure out each of these discounts?
   a. 10 percent?   b. 25 percent?   c. 50 percent?
   How did you figure out the fractions?

3. Which item has been discounted by the largest **percentage**?

4. Which item do you think has been discounted by the largest **amount**? Explain your reasoning.

5. Suppose you wanted to buy the bike helmet. How could you figure out:
   a. the amount it is being discounted?   b. the sale price?

6. Calculate the discount and the sale price for each item in the advertisement.

In Viewville, 400,000 people watched T.V. between the hours of 7 p.m. and 9 p.m. on May 3. The chart below shows which channels they chose.

PERCENTAGE OF VIEWING AUDIENCE			
	7 p.m. to 8 p.m.	8 p.m. to 9 p.m.	9 p.m. to 10 p.m.
Channel 4	10%	15%	20%
Channel 6	9%	19%	18%
Channel 8	32%	16%	8%
Channel 9	29%	25%	24%
Other channels	20%	25%	30%

1. Which T.V. channel do you think had the most popular show? In what time slot was the show aired?

2. How many people viewed Channel 4 between:
   a. 7 p.m. and 8 p.m.?
   b. 8 p.m. and 9 p.m.?
   c. 9 p.m. and 10 p.m.?
   How did you figure out your answers?

3. **Estimate** the number of people who viewed Channel 6 in each of the 3 time slots. How did you make your estimates?

4. Look at the percentages for Channel 8.
   a. How did the size of the viewing audience change from one time slot to the next? How do you know?
   b. Estimate the size of the viewing audience for each time slot.

5. In which time slot do you think Channel 9 had 96,000 viewers? How do you know?

Cathy is the owner of a café that is full at breakfast and lunchtime. She drew this plan and recorded the maximum number her café could seat.

SEATING PLAN

10 at the counter
7 per booth
6 per large table
4 per small table

□ small table   □ large table   □ booth   ● counter seats

1. What is the maximum number that can be seated at one time in Cathy's Café?

2. Cathy serves breakfast from 6 a.m. to 8:30 a.m. She knows that each customer spends about $5.50 and is seated for about 30 minutes. Estimate:
   a. the number of breakfast customers Cathy has each day
   b. Cathy's daily breakfast sales.
   Explain how you made your estimates.
   Was there more than one way to estimate?

3. Cathy serves lunch from 11 a.m. to 2 p.m. She knows that each customer spends about $7.50 and is seated for about 45 minutes. Estimate:
   a. the number of lunch customers Cathy has each day
   b. Cathy's daily lunch sales.
   Explain how you made your estimates.

Cathy read her staff's time cards for the last week of May.

Head Chef: *Bryan*	On	Off
Mon.	5:40 am	2:20 pm
Tue.	5:50 am	1:55 pm
Wed.	5:40 am	1:55 pm
Thur.	5:35 am	2:20 pm
Fri.	5:25 am	2:45 pm

Assistant Chef: *Deanne*	On	Off
Mon.	5:50 am	1:45 pm
Tue.	5:40 am	2:15 pm
Wed.	5:55 am	2:05 pm
Thur.	5:40 am	2:10 pm
Fri.	5:30 am	2:15 pm

Kitchen Assistant: *Lucia*	On	Off
Mon.	6:00 am	1:45 pm
Tue.	5:55 am	1:55 pm
Wed.	5:55 am	2:00 pm
Thur.	5:45 am	2:05 pm
Fri.	5:45 am	2:15 pm

Dish Washer: *Pat*	On	Off
Mon.	6:30 am	2:15 pm
Tue.	6:30 am	2.20 pm
Wed.	6:30 am	2:20 pm
Thur.	6:30 am	2:30 pm
Fri.	6:25 am	2:40 pm

1. Look at Bryan's time card.
   a. About how many hours did Bryan work on Monday?
   b. On which day did Bryan work the longest hours?
      How did you decide?

2. Cathy wanted answers to these questions:
   a. What was the total time worked in the kitchen on Monday?
   b. What was the total time Bryan worked that week?
      Estimate the answers to Cathy's questions.
      Then explain what you did.

3. Cathy needed to find out how much to pay her
   kitchen staff at the end of the week. Copy the chart,
   and then calculate:
   a. the time worked by each person
   b. the amount each person should be paid
   c. the total amount paid.

	May 25-29: Kitchen Staff Wages			
	Bryan	Deanne	Lucia	Pat
Hourly rate of pay	$14.80	$11.40	$7.20	$5.20
Number of hours worked (to nearest $\frac{1}{4}$ hour)				
Weekly pay				

Cathy made pie graphs to show the popularity of different kinds of juice sold at breakfast and at lunch.

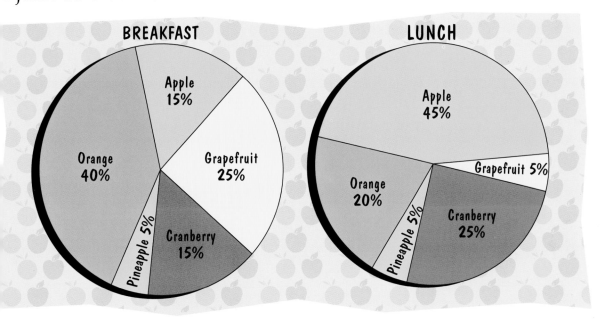

. Look at the breakfast graph.
   a. What **percentage** of the juice sold was orange juice?
   b. What **fraction** of the juice sold was orange juice?
   c. Write the fraction of juice sold that was:
   • grapefruit   • apple   • cranberry   • pineapple.

. Look at the lunch graph. Write the fraction of juice sold that was:
   • orange   • apple   • cranberry   • pineapple   • grapefruit.

. Suppose Cathy sold 60 glasses of juice at breakfast and 40 glasses of juice at lunch.
   a. What **fraction** of the total juice sold was orange juice? Explain how you figured it out.
   b. Use what you found out to help you figure out what **percentage** of the juice was orange juice.
   c. Figure out the **percentage** of total juice that was:
   • grapefruit   • apple   • cranberry   • pineapple.

Bryan and Deanne used this graph to help them order some of the ingredients for their famous oatmeal cakes.

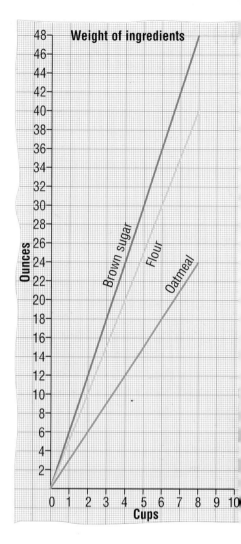

1. Look at the graph.
   What information does it show?
   How do you think Bryan and Deanne used the graph?

2. Use the graph to find the answers to these questions.
   a. What is the weight of 4 cups of:
      • oatmeal?   • flour?
      • brown sugar?
      How did you find out?
   b. What is the weight of one cup of:
      • oatmeal?   • flour?
      • brown sugar?
   c. How does the weight of the brown sugar compare to the weight of the oatmeal?

3. About how many cups of each ingredient could you get from one pound? Explain how you made your estimates.

4. Suppose a recipe for oatmeal cakes calls for 1 cup of flour, $\frac{1}{2}$ cup of brown sugar, and $1\frac{1}{2}$ cups of oatmeal.
   a. What weight of each of those ingredients would Bryan and Deanne need for 6 batches?
   b. Bryan and Deanne buy ingredients in **whole pounds**. How many pounds of flour, brown sugar, and oatmeal would they buy for 6 batches? Explain your answer.